MARCO

MADEIRA

Sightseeing Highlights

The green volcanic island in the middle of the Atlantic has much to offer: craggy mountain tops and wildly romantic coasts, unique laurasilva woods and a fantastic profusion of flowers, picturesque hamlets and a charming capital city – we have put together what you definitely should not miss.

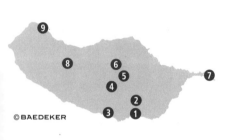

© BAEDEKER

❶ ✶✶ Funchal

Madeira's capital entices with flowering parks, museums, a cathedral that is equally modest and impressive, the harbour and a lively old city.
page 141

❷ ✶✶ Monte

Visit the Jardím Tropical and the pilgrimage church in this mountain village. Take the cable car up from Funchal and get shaken up in a basket sled on the way back down.
page 169

❸ ✶✶ Cabo Girão

At Cabo Girão enjoy the view from one of the highest coastal cliffs in the world, provided you aren't afraid of heights, since the drop is almost 600m/2000ft.
page 133

❹ ✶✶ Curral das Freiras

The »nuns' barn« is surrounded by mountains and situated in a valley. The approaching drive gives a breathtaking view of it from above.
page 138

❺ ✶✶ Pico do Arieiro

The convenient road leads almost to the peak and gives less experienced hikers the chance to enjoy Madeira's outstanding views.
page 178

❻ ✶✶ Pico Ruivo

The hike from Pico do Arieiro to
Pico Ruivo, Madeira's highest
mountain, takes about four hours.
The panoramic views are overwhelming. **page 178**

❼ ✶✶ Ponta de São Lourenço

Madeira's eastern point is rocky
and rough. The rock exposed by
rock slides document the volcanic
origins of the island – a play of
colours in ochre, red, black and
blue. **page 181**

❽ ✶✶ Paúl da Serra

The barren green expanse here
could almost be in Scotland.
page 172

❾ ✶✶ Porto Moniz

When lava sizzles and splashes as
it falls into the ocean and wind
and waves batter it for millenia,
rock formations can form that even
have practical use – as natural sea
water swimming pools.
page 185

Do You Feel Like ...

... experiences in, at and under water or insight into the past and the island's interior? Like breathtaking enchantment and conditions? Like culture, fashion and artisan work? Recommendations for your personal Madeira experience:

WATER WORLDS

- **Golden beach ...**
  ... is rare on Madeira, but sand was brought from Morocco to form beaches at Calheta and Machico.
  pages 124, 168
- **Deep sea feeling light** ▶
  Visitors to the Aquário da Madeira feel like divers – at one place they can even look up at the sea creatures.
  page 187
- **Vertical water**
  Canyoning adventure for everyone who like Abseiling in wet canyons.
  page 103
- **Large sea creatures**
  On a ride on the »Ribeira Brava« dolphins and even whales can be watched. An alternative: the whaling museum in Caniçal.
  page 72, 135

CULTURE

- **Modern architecture**
  The cultural centre Centro das Artes – Casa das Mudas in Calheta and the hotel The Vine in Funchal are examples of recent developments in architecture on the island.
  page 126, 150
- **Classical music**
  The Madeira music festival in June offers ten days of classical music in various places in and around Funchal.
  page 77
- ◀ **20th century art**
  In the Fortaleza de São Tiago in Funchal there is a small selection of Portuguese modern art; Centro das Artes – Casa das Mudas in Calheta exhibits a collection of Art déco.
  pages 125, 153

INSIGHT

BREATHTAKING

TEXTILES

BACKGROUND

PRICE CATEGORIES
Restaurants
(for a main dish)
€€€€ = over €20
€€€ = €14–€20
€€ = €8–€14
€ = up to €8
Hotels (for a double room)
€€€€ = over €110
€€€ = €70–€110
€€ = €40–€70
€ = up to €40

Note
Billable service numbers are marked with an asterisk:
*0180....

ENJOY MADEIRA

TOURS

Basket sled drivers in Monte waiting for brave passengers

SIGHTS FROM A TO Z

Lush flowers in a Madeira garden

PRACTICAL INFORMATION

Fruit and vegetables galore
in the Funchal market ha

BACKGROUND

In this section you will find all sorts of interesting information about this lush volcanic island in the Atlantic Ocean, about its history and culture, its economy and politics as well as everyday life on the island that attracts visitors all year round because of its mild climate and magnificent vegetation.

Flower Island in the Atlantic...

...is just one of the many colourful names given to this former bridgehead between the Old and the New World. »Daughter of the volcano«, »bride of the wind« or »island of eternal spring« Madeira is also called. Madeira lies almost twice as far away from its Portuguese motherland as from the coast of the African continent.

»Public amusements are wholly lacking«, wrote the author of a Handbook for Madeira in 1885, while giving fulsome praise to the mild climate, magnificent landscape and generous hospitality of the islanders. That has not changed much, and the recreational opportunities have in turn increased beyond measure.

Madeira's average temperature of around 20°C/68°F, even in the November to February period, makes it a popular holiday destination for the winter months in Europe. A fantastic natural landscape, rich in vegetation and floral splendour throughout the year, attracts visitors searching for relaxation. Ancient laurisilva woodland and luxuriant gardens, white surf crashing on the coastline, deep valleys, rugged mountains and lush, green uplands create a fascinating ensemble.

To the northeast, the neighbouring island of Porto Santo offers an interesting contrast, with over 9km/5mi of sandy beaches instead of floral resplendence and high mountains. It is relatively sparse but is very suitable for beach holidays. The Ilhas Desertas to the southeast have been a designated nature reserve since 1990, off limits to visitors.

Madeira, the famous sweet wine from the Atlantic island

A HIKERS' PARADISE

The hike along the levadas is very beautiful. The Irrigation channels constructed here over centuries were not laid with hikers in mind, but for the levadeiros, the men who tend the levadas. However, today they are perfectly suited for hiking and reconnoitring Madeira's original landscape and its diverse regions. A good head for heights and sturdy legs are helpful and the right equipment is advisable, as the steep mountainside is unguarded at some points, or it may be necessary to balance on the levada wall. The reward for such endeavours comes in the form of spectacular views!

FUNCHAL, THE HUB OF ACTIVITIES

The capital city of Funchal, located on the south coast, is the cultural and tourist centre of the island. Although it is the seat of government, centre for shopping, a bishop's seat, a university town and a port, the site of engaging museums, tropical gardens and amusements, this is no overcrowded metropolis. Nevertheless, in the western part of town, a veritable hotel zone has developed, whilst new settlements have crept up the slopes of Funchal Bay and traffic has drastically increased in the city centre.

ALL ON ONE ISLAND

New roads, constructed in recent years with the assistance of EU funding, now connect Funchal with relative ease to previously remote regions such as the north coast or the western promontory of the island. There is much worth discovering in those regions too: welcoming fishing communities with small harbours, village churches that glory in Baroque opulence, small thatched houses, fortifications to thwart pirates, mansions – known as quintas – at the heart of magnificent parks, terraced fields with grapevines for the famous Madeira wine, banana plantations and lava caves. Traditional handicrafts live on in ornate Madeira embroidery and basketry. Pictures made from azulejos – ceramic tiles – adorn façades, whilst plaster mosaics of light and dark stones add atmosphere to Funchal and many other places on the island. If there were a guest book for Madeira, it would read like a »Who's Who« of the noble, rich and beautiful classes. Winston Churchill whiled away his time drawing and painting in the harbour of Câmara de Lobos, George Bernard Shaw sampled the delights of the tango against a tropical backdrop, and Empress Elisabeth I of Austria came here to escape the cold Viennese winter. Discover your very own, personal slice of paradise on Madeira, the island of eternal spring!

Facts

Natural Environment

The nature and scenery on this small island group is absolutely spectacular. Everything from impressive mountain scenery, stunningly rugged coastlines to desert-like landscapes can be found on these volcanic islands in the Atlantic. The main island Madeira, the »island of eternal spring«, owes its lush vegetation to the extreme yet warm Atlantic climate.

BORN OF FIRE

The Madeira archipelago (Arquipélago da Madeira) is situated in the Atlantic, some 500km/300mi to the west of the Moroccan coast. The main island of Madeira rises out of the Atlantic Ocean from a depth of 4000–5000m/13,000–16,000ft to as high as 1862m/6100ft above sea level (Pico Ruivo, »Red Peak«). Also part of the archipelago are the island of Porto Santo at a distance of 43km/26mi, the Ilhas Desertas – Ilhéu Chão, Deserta Grande and Ilhéu do Bugio – approximately 20km/13mi southeast, and the five tiny Ilhas Selvagens (covering approx. 4 sq km/1.5 sq mi together), much further south, closer to the Canary Isles.

Archipelago in the Atlantic

The first impression for newcomers to Madeira is striking: In places where the lush and colourful vegetation does not flourish, black and brown lava cliffs, dark basalt and light volcanic tuff dominate the island, where fissured rock faces climb almost vertically from the sea in a landscape of sharp ridges, abruptly plunging gorges and immense rocky cliffs, such as the 580m/1900ft-high Cabo Girão. Cooled lava streams at Porto Moniz and the lava drips in the caves at São Vicente are also noteworthy. Seawater and wind have shaped the highly unusual northeastern promontory of Madeira, Ponta de São Lourenço, hollowing out the volcanic tuff stone over the centuries to form gradually disintegrating caves, the characteristic »tafonis«. Solidified lava has been hewn into sharp-edged cliffs, often inaccessible to all except to the seagulls that breed there.

Volcanic islands

> **? Size comparison**
>
> MARCO POLO INSIGHT
>
> With its 741 square kilometres (286 sq mi), the Madeira archipelago covers about the same area as the city of Hamburg in Germany.

Madeira, Porto Santo and the Ilhas Desertas, together with the Azores, the Cape Verde islands and the Canaries, comprise the

Origins of the archipelago

Sugarcane made Madeirans wealthy in the 15th century

Volcanic Island

That Madeira is of volcanic origin can be seen in the rock formations of the barren, rocky eastern tip of Ponta de São Lourenço, the lava caves in São Vicente and the lava-rock pools in Porto Moniz. The highest peaks of the central mountainous area formed by volcanic activities and upward folding of the earth's crust rise in the west and gradually merge into the high plateau Paúl da Serra. Both the north coast, which drops steeply into the ocean in most places, and the coastal areas in the south, which are less rugged and more suitable for agriculture, add to the diversity of this interesting and beautiful island.

❶ Ponta do Pargo
A red-capped lighthouse marks the end of the island to the west. Beyond it is just the vast blue ocean.

❷ Porto Moniz
Lava cliffs, witnesses to furious volcanic activity hundreds of thousands of years ago, shaped and moulded by the ever-surging waves and winds, make this landscape so stunningly beautiful.

❸ São Vicente
In the lava caves, formed about 890,000 years ago, you will see solidified lava drops hanging from the ceilings of the caves. The Centre for Volcanism offers information on the formation history.

❹ Paúl da Serra
Fog, wind and rain have formed this high plateau, which at first glance might seem somewhat uninteresting, but a closer look reveals how it stands in stunning contrast to the high mountain range nearby.

❺ Pico do Ruivo
Madeira's highest mountain (1862m/ 109ft above sea level) has something for everyone, even for alpinists – a rugged mountain world with its peaks reaching for the sky and its deep canyons with their steep and imposing cliffs draws visitors into its spell.

❻ Ponta de São Lourenço
The colourful rock layers on the eastern end of Madiera are hardened lava streams of various ages.

❼ Curral das Freiras
In the past, it was mistakenly believed that the valley basin of Curral das Freiras was a volcanic crater, but the assumption these days is that it was formed by extended erosive activity.

❽ Cabo Girão
One of the highest sea cliffs in the world can be found on the small island of Madeira. Best not to have a fear of heights here.

Tree heath and laurel: two of the indigenous plants near Ribeira da Janela

Macaronesia Islands, otherwise known as the mid-Atlantic volcanic islands. Today, they lie far from the volcanically active Atlantic Ridge at the border of the Atlantic Ocean's crust. Between 135 and 160 million years ago, however, as the Atlantic Ocean gradually began to open up, the submerged volcanic ridge exactly followed the line along which the Macaronesian Islands now reach up from the waters. In actual fact, the islands visible today only appeared above sea level much later, some 10 to 40 million years ago. At first, beneath the ocean, surface rifts and chasms opened, out of which basaltic magma erupted, created vast bodies of basaltic lava. Ten to twenty million years ago, these undersea volcanoes rose above the ocean surface, forming volcanic islands with basalt stacks, cinder cones and lava streams. Saltwater and the elements weathered the young volcanic islands as the process of erosion began. Around seven million years ago, a renewed phase of violent volcanic activity saw Porto Santo rise above sea level.

Current situation

Volcanic activity in the region of the Madeira archipelago has since decreased considerably, but is far from over. In 2001, scientists from the Meteor research group discovered and mapped a submarine volcanic ridge structure approximately 50km/30mi west of Madeira. It is conjectured that a so-called »**hot spot**« exists in the area of the Madeira archipelago, periodically responsible for fresh outbreaks of volcanic activity. Here, the sea bed drifts over a fixed magma flue »hot spot«, which penetrates the earth's crust like a welding torch, piling up huge cones of volcanic matter on the ocean floor. The Madeira »hot spot« has now been charted in the region of the Madeira archipelago, tracing the movement of the African Plate as it shifts northeast, towards Europe.

Landscapes on Madeira and Porto Santo

The spine of the **main island of Madeira** is a mountain range of jagged and precipitous ridges, stretching from east to west. In the western part of the island lies the Paúl da Serra tableland; to the east is the smaller plateau of Santo António da Serra. On the north and south slopes of the central chain, sheer rock faces surround basins which then open into the ocean as deep incisions or gorges. Especially on the northern coast, it is easy to see the frequent alternation of ash and lava strata. The coasts of Madeira are steep and rocky; narrow expanses of sand can only be found on a few erstwhile lava streams flowing into the ocean.

Porto Santo, by way of contrast, consists mainly of sandy uplands with volcanic cones as high as 517m/1696ft. The volcanic rock of the Ilhas Desertas reaches a height of 479m/1570ft. Attempts to put this dry and infertile land to agricultural use were swiftly abandoned: hence the name meaning »Deserted Islands«.

CLIMATE

Madeira owes its lush vegetation to a climate that is markedly oceanic and, as a result of its low latitude, warm. Depressions from northern latitudes determine the winter weather, whilst the northeast trade winds dominate the summer half of the year, creating stark climatic differences between the windward side to the north and the lee side to the south. This is caused by the formation of clouds, as northerly winds bring damp air masses which gather around the mountains, primarily in the mornings.

From around noon, the air masses warm up and begin to rise, thus influencing the weather on the southern part of the island.

Island of »eternal spring«

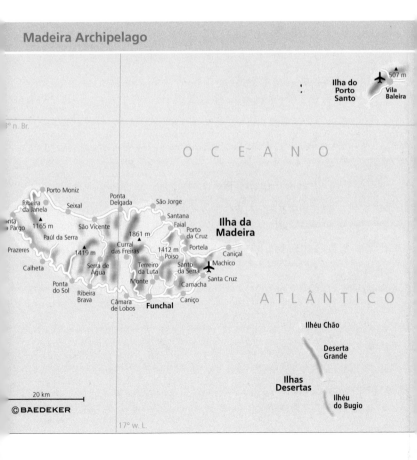

Madeira Archipelago

North and
south side

On the northern side, where the trade winds are caught on the mountainsides, rainfall is heavy, especially in the winter months. On the southern side of the island, annual precipitation averages are much lower. Apart from the remarkably dry months of July and August, showers can fall at any moment on Madeira, with longer periods of rainfall quite possible further inland. The annual mean temperature on the island is also determined by its geographical location at 32° latitude. Even in winter, it is rare for the thermometer to drop below 18°C/64°F in the lower regions of the island during the day. Snowfall is a distinct possibility in the uplands, but the snow never settles.

There is a difference between the north and south: Whilst the annual mean temperature in Funchal is 18.2°C/64.5°F, the damper northern side at Ponta Delgada registers just 17.4°C/63°F. Occasional masses of hot air from the Sahara make their way to Madeira; these winds can be unpleasant, bringing not only hot air with them but desert sand as well. Water temperatures vary between 14°C/57°F in March and around 22°C/71°F at the height of summer.

FLORA AND FAUNA

Primeval
forest

When João Gonçalves Zarco and Tristão Vaz Teixeira set foot on Madeira in 1419 and were confronted with a mountainous, densely forested and impassable island, they christened the place with a name befitting the terrain: Madeira means wood in Portuguese. The discoverers initially settled on the flatter neighbouring island of Porto Santo, using it as a base from which to explore the main island. Early Portuguese settlers opted for fire clearance as their preferred method of claiming the land. According to contemporary documentation, the fires burned for seven years, with little remaining of the primeval forest which had grown over centuries. This destroyed the majority of the indigenous flora and fauna.

Vegetation
today

»Flor do Oceano« – »Flower of the Ocean« – is what the Portuguese call their island in the Atlantic today. The vegetation of Madeira is nowadays characterized by a tropical abundance of splendid and useful plants from all corners of the earth, thanks to its mild climate, plentiful winter rainfall and the artificial irrigation system of the levadas, which channel water from the mountains to the fields and gardens along the coast. As well as pine and European broadleaf, countless evergreen trees and shrubs of tropical and subtropical origin thrive here, such as palms, monkey puzzle, hickory, cork oak, camphor and fig trees, papaya, palm lily, yuccas, medlar, mimosa eucalyptus, bamboo, papyrus plants, cyatheales and agave. Many streets are lined with blossoming hydrangeas, usually blue in colour,

agapanthus in white and blue, and bel-
ladonna lilies (Brunsvigia rosea), originally from South Africa. **Orchids** are
cultivated in many varieties in orchid
gardens. A visit to such a cultivation
centre is commonly a disappointment,
as the various species bloom at different
times and are relatively unspectacular in
appearance out of season. Orchids are,
however, hugely popular as enduring
and low-maintenance souvenirs. In the
gardens of Funchal, often contained

within high walls, an enchanting floral richness can be enjoyed in
winter and more especially in spring: roses, camellias, rhododen-
drons, azaleas, pelargoniums, begonias, bignonias, daturas, bougainvillea, wisteria and many more. Indigenous to Mexico, the poinsettia
now flowers prodigiously on Madeira. The **strelitzia** (bird of paradise), introduced to Madeira from South Africa in 1778, can be
found in almost every garden and is grown in fields for export. Its
striking blossoms, resembling birds' heads, are carefully packed as
popular souvenirs.

Crop plants

Upwards of 800m/2600ft, the prevailing **eucalyptus woods** have
been developed through reforestation. Both species, Eucalyptus glob-
ulus and Eucalyptus ficifolia, originate from the Australian continent
and were only exported to Europe in the 20th century. The eucalyptus
tree is highly valued as a rapidly renewable wood with many uses. A
hike through the forests is all the more pleasant when the inimitable
eucalyptus scent fills the air, a eucalyptus twig in the car is a natural
air freshener, and tasty sweets can be manufactured from its essential
oils. The downside: eucalyptus draws large quantities of water from
the ground in the wider surrounding area. At the time of Madeira's
discovery, Florence fennel (Foeniculum dulce) was widespread on
the island. The name of Funchal is a reminder of the fact: Portuguese
seafarers who landed in the bay are said to have been so beguiled by
its aroma that they named the town after it. Today fennel is used for
seasoning and also to make sweets. The most important crops are
grapes, potatoes and bananas. Aloe vera is gaining in economic significance as well (▶p. 35).

Remains of
laurisilva
forest

Only a small area of the original **laurisilva forest**, so prevalent in
the Mesozoic age and in the Mediterranean too, has survived on
Madeira, the Canaries, the Azores and Cape Verde Islands. In 1999
the woodland was declared a **UNESCO World Heritage** site, forming the heart of a nature reserve. The laurel woods contain sizeable
numbers of Madeira laurel (Laurus indica), stinkwood or till trees

Island of Eternal Spring

Thanks to the mild climate Madeira, the flower of the sea, blooms all year round. Spring and fall, however, are the main blossoming seasons.

▶ **Year-round blossoms**
Many flowers bloom all year round, e.g. African senna, bird of paradise, anthurium, bougainvillea, begonia, morning glory, hibiscus and cape plumbago.

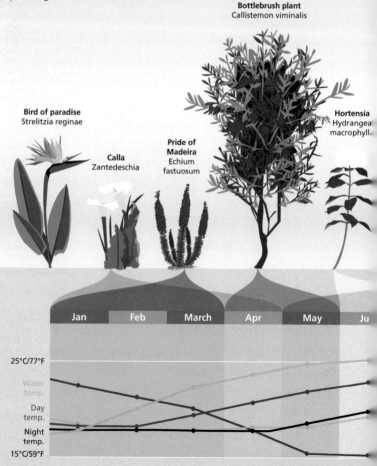

Bottlebrush plant
Callistemon viminalis

Bird of paradise
Strelitzia reginae

Calla
Zantedeschia

Pride of Madeira
Echium fastuosum

Hortensia
Hydrangea macrophylla

| Jan | Feb | March | Apr | May | Ju |

25°C/77°F

Water temp.

Day temp.

Night temp.

15°C/59°F

► Unique

More than 150 of the more than 1200 varieties of plants on Madeira are endemic; that means that they grow nowhere else in the world.

One of the rarest of these is the Madeira cranesbill. It is native to central Madeira, where it grows in small populations on humus or fresh soil. It blooms from March until May.

Varieties of flowers and plants in Portugal (with endemic plants in %)

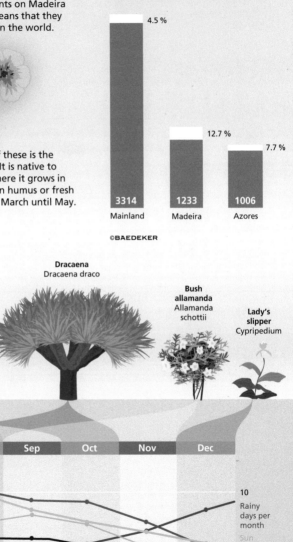

4.5 %	12.7 %	7.7 %
3314	1233	1006
Mainland	Madeira	Azores

©BAEDEKER

Oleander
Nerium oleander

Dracaena
Dracaena draco

Bush allamanda
Allamanda schottii

Lady's slipper
Cypripedium

July	Aug	Sep	Oct	Nov	Dec

10

Rainy days per month

Sun hours per day

0

When do they bloom?

African tulip tree	September/October
Agapanthus	May – September
Agave	December – March
Aloe	October – February
Angel's trumpet	April/May
Anthurium (Flamingo plant)	all year
Aralia	July – November
Banana	all year
Bird of paradise	all year
Bottlebrush	April – June
Brunfelsia	twice a year (spring and fall)
Calla	January – April
Camelia	December – May
Castor oil plant	all year
Cattleya	February – October
Citron	February – April
Clivia	April – June
Coral tree	January – March
Cymbidium (orchid)	February – May
Eucalyptus	August – December

Fennel	July – September
Frangipani	June – October
Hibiscus	almost all year (main bloom in summer)
Hortensia	June – September
Hyacinth	March/April
Ice plant	March – August
Jacaranda	April – June
Jimson weed	all year
Judas tree	March – May
Magnolia	May – August
Mimosa	December – March
Morning glory	all year
Pampas grass	August – October
Poinsettia	October – February
Pride of Madeira	May – July
Protea	May – December
Oleander	May – September
Opuntia (prickly pear)	May – July
Rhododendron	May – July
Wisteria	March – May

? Worth knowing about Laurel

There are four types of laurel on Madeira: At 40 m/131 ft, the stinkwood or till tree is the tallest, the wood of the Canary laurel is used to make aromatic skewers for grilling, the azores laurel is used as a spice and the reddish wood of the Madeira laurel is used for furniture.

(Oreodaphne foetens) and laurel or Canary laurel (Laurus barbusano). Above 1000m/3300ft, Canary Islands juniper (Juniperus cedrus), wild olive trees (Olea maderensis), above 1500m/4900ft Scotch heather (Erica scoparia) and shield fern (Polystichum falcinellum) can be found. The **dragon tree** (Dracaena draco), probably the island's most distinctive indigenous plant, has largely disappeared as a consequence of the multiple uses for its wood. More recently, it has increasingly been planted in parks and gardens for decorative purposes.

Animal kingdom Of the many varieties in Madeira's bird kingdom, only 14 or 15 breeds are natives of the island. Some 200 bird species live or breed on Madeira, including birds of prey such as buzzards and falcons, along with canaries, the Madeiran wood pigeon and petrels. Magpies, chaffinches, common buzzards, the rare Madeira laurel pigeon and the Madeira firecrest, a member of the wren family – also known as »bisbis« on account of its characteristic call – all inhabit the laurel forest. These dwindling bird populations in the laurel forest are the very ones threatened with extinction. The highest share of indigenous species can be found amongst the insects. In adapting, many have lost the ability to fly. The poisonous wolf spider (Geolycosa ingens) is endemic to the island of Deserta Grande, a nature reserve with no access for tourists. The only reptile species is the Madeira wall lizard, which likes to feed on ripe fruit in gardens and plantations, in spite of the efforts of farmers to prevent it from doing so. Snakes do not live on the islands. Bats are the only indigenous mammals.

Introduced farm and wild animals Cattle, horses, donkeys, goats, pigs, sheep, hedgehogs and rabbits, as well as rats and mice, were all brought to the archipelago by man. Rainbow trout farms have also been introduced, the trout reared in hatcheries (in Ribeiro Frio, for example) and later released into streams for anglers' enjoyment.

In the sea The waters around Madeira are very deep, so fish are not especially common. This is not a habitat suitable for the marine life found in brackish or shallower water elsewhere in the world, such as mussels

Crops are even grown on the smallest of terraces,
which are hard to till without machinery

Black scabbardfish live in the deep of the ocean

or crabs. Tuna, monkfish, redfish and octopus live in the waters surrounding Madeira. The most important edible fish of Madeira is the **black scabbardfish** (»espada preta«), an eel-like, scaleless deep-sea fish up to 2m/6ft in length and found only around Madeira and off the coast of Japan. It lives over 1000m/3300ft below sea level, climbing to just 800m/2600ft at night, when it may be caught on long fishing lines. In the service of gastronomy, it suffers a gruesome death: As water pressure decreases the closer it gets to the surface, its air bladder, gills and eyes burst and its slimy, scaleless skin turns black. Hauled upwards, the colourful iridescence it displays in its natural habitat is lost, with only the black dyes surviving.

A large **monk seal** (Monachus monachus, ▶MARCO POLO Insight, p.130) population, now almost extinct, used to thrive in the bay of Câmara de Lobos and was also prevalent around the Canary Islands, on the northwest coast of Africa and the Mediterranean in former times. To ensure the colony's survival, as well as to protect the marine flora and fauna of the Madeira archipelago, nature reserves have been created, also encompassing the Ilhas Desertas and Ilhas Selvagens. Immediately off Madeira, the Ponta do Garajau at the eastern side of the Bay of Funchal was given partial protection in 1986 and fishing has been heavily restricted. Diving equipment is necessary to explore the magnificent underwater regions of the nature reserve. Grouper, among others, can be seen here, andmantas also venture into these waters from time to time. Through the efforts of the local population, the strip of coast at Rocha do Navio has been designated a conservation area, offering a potential habitat to monk seals. Today, roughly two thirds of Madeira has been awarded nature reserve status for the protection of endemic fauna and flora.

Population · Politics · Economy

Madeira belongs to Portugal but was given the status of an autonomous region and therefore has a high level of political autonomy in matters of internal affairs. The island's economy relies mainly on tourism.

POPULATION

On account of its more favourable climate, the south coast of Madeira is more densely populated than the rest of the island. Funchal alone with some 130,000 inhabitants represents half of the population. As the island's main tourist centre, Funchal offers greater potential to earn money than elsewhere on Madeira. The extended family used to be a typical feature of the Madeiran population structure, but today families with many children are becoming rarer. Population growth is stagnating in line with Portugal in general.

Madeirans

Tourism may be on the increase, but this cannot disguise the fact that young people, in particular those with good qualifications, are faced with limited career opportunities. This is borne out by a high migration rate, with many young adults heading for the Portuguese mainland or other European countries on completing their education. Popular overseas destinations include Brazil and Venezuela as Portuguese and Spanish-speaking countries respectively, as well as South Africa, USA and Canada.

High migration rate

At the university in Funchal, founded in 1988, the emphasis is on natural sciences, for example marine biology; degrees in art and design or music and languages are also possible.

University

The Roman Catholic Church is gradually losing the great influence it once held over the population, especially with regard to the young people living in and around Funchal. Outside the capital, the church

Religion

Welcome to Everyday Life

If you would like to experience Madeira not only as a tourist but would also enjoy meeting the islanders, below are some of the ways to do just that.

FESTAS, FEIRAS, MERCADOS

Madeira's residents love to celebrate. At village, saint and harvest festivals as well as at agricultural fairs or at farmers' markets it's easy to meet the locals, whether you saunter over to the vendor with the famous grilled beef skewers or check out the raffle stand, buy vegetables or homemade bread. *Sunday market in Prazeres (8 am to 5 pm, in the hall); Agricultural Fair Feira Agropecuária/Feira do Gado (one weekend in July or August, on the exhibition grounds in the woods between Ponta do Pargo and Porto Moniz); Agricultural Fair Festa do Limão (Lemon Festival, Ilha/ Santana, mid-May); Festa da Cereja (Cherry Festival, Câmara de Lobos, Jardim da Serra, mid/end June); Festa da Banana (Madalena do Mar, end of July)*

LIVE WITH THE LOCALS

Some of the historical summer residences on the island are still family-owned, but they have been converted into guesthouses. The same was done with many of the small townhouses and other private homes. Sometimes the owners themselves (still) tend to their properties and/or their guests, and they usually have many colourful stories to tell, about anything and everything, from what's happening on the island these days but also about its history. The locals usually speak English quite well – and you will probably even meet some former citizens of the United Kingdom who now live on the island. *In an enchanted garden across from the monastery of the same name is the Residencial Santa Clara guesthouse (14 rooms, Rua da Calçada do Pico, 16 B, Tel. 2 91 74 21 94).*

ENJOY NATIVITY SCENES

In many of Madeira's communities, a large nativity scene, some with real animals, draws the locals in droves at Christmas time. Some villages have nativity scene competitions and the residents are very proud to present their sometimes room-filling and a little tacky yet amusingly bizarre »lapinhas«. The jury and visitors are usually provided with beverages and snacks.

Information through the local parish/church office; the nativity scenes are usually on display until 12 January (Santo Amaro).

HIKING WITH THE AMIGOS DA NATUREZA

Madeira's Friends of Nature Club organizes 1 to 3 hiking tours (10–16 km/6–10 mi) a month from January through December to various regions of the island. The bus of the Amigos da Natureza leaves around 7.45 am from Avenida do Mar (near the cable car station). Early reservation required.

Amigos da Natureza
Tel. 2 91 23 76 27
Mobile 9 62 31 54 57
www.amigosdanatureza.pt.to

LEARN PORTUGUESE

Funchal, Machico, Santa Cruz und Estreito de Câmara de Lobos have language schools where you can learn Portuguese or take advanced classes. Native speakers teach in small groups of up to four or on an individual basis.

Academia de Línguas da Madeira
Rua do Ribeirinho de Baixo 33-B 2°
9050-447 Funchal
Tel. 2 91 23 10 69
Mobile: 9 66 91 24 24 / 9 13 80 46 68
http://alm-madeira.com

CENTRO COMMERCIAL

Madeirans love huge shopping malls that offer almost everything under one roof, including restaurants, cinemas and fun activities for children. Whole families, couples, groups of friends, young or old, all linger for hours in this colourful mix of department stores, supermarkets and boutiques. The malls are usually open until 10 pm and until midnight on the weekends.

Dolce Vita (www.dolcevita.pt, located centrally on Rua Dr. Brito Câmara); Madeira Shopping-Center (www. madeirashopping.pt, in the Santo António district); Forum Madeira (www. forummadeira.com, with rooftop garden, on Estrada Monumental)

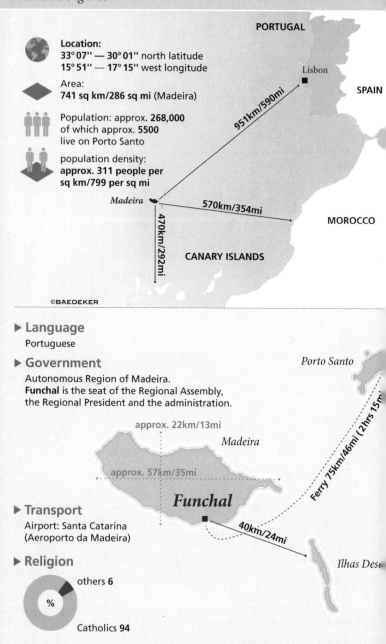

Location:
33° 07'' — 30° 01'' north latitude
15° 51'' — 17° 15'' west longitude

Area:
741 sq km/286 sq mi (Madeira)

Population: approx. 268,000
of which approx. 5500
live on Porto Santo

population density:
**approx. 311 people per
sq km/799 per sq mi**

PORTUGAL

Lisbon

SPAIN

951km/590mi

Madeira

570km/354mi

MOROCCO

470km/292mi

CANARY ISLANDS

©BAEDEKER

▶ **Language**
Portuguese

▶ **Government**
Autonomous Region of Madeira.
Funchal is the seat of the Regional Assembly,
the Regional President and the administration.

Porto Santo

approx. 22km/13mi

Madeira

approx. 57km/35mi

Funchal

Ferry 75km/46mi (2hrs 15m...

▶ **Transport**
Airport: Santa Catarina
(Aeroporto da Madeira)

40km/24mi

Ilhas Dese...

▶ **Religion**

others **6**

%

Catholics **94**

▶ Economy

The most important source of income is **tourism** with more than **800,000 visitors** per year.

The majority of the guests come from the UK and Germany. In the summer many Portuguese from the mainland visit the island.

Main export products:

Bananas
(approx. 15,000 t per year)

Wine
(approx. 3.4 mil. litres per year)

▶ Climate

MAXIMUM

25.7

20 °C   19.1

SEA

18.9

MINIMUM

10 °C   13.1

J F M A M J J A S O N D

Precipitation

in days per month

8 9 7 5 3 2 0 1 3 6 8 9

in hours per day

5 5 6 6 7 5 7 8 7 6 5 5

J F M A M J J A S O N D

▶ Islands in the Atlantic Ocean

Las Palmas

Santa Cruz de Tenerife

Praia

Funchal

Ponta Delgada

	Santiago	*Madeira*	*Gran Canaria*	*Tenerife*	*São Miguel*
	Cap Verde Archipelago	Madeira Archipelago	Canary Islands	Canary Islands	Azore Islands
Area in sq km/ sqmi	991/382	741/286	1560/602	2034/785	747/288
Population	290,000	268,000	850,000	907,000	140,000
Highest elevation	Pico de Fogo **2829m/9281ft**	Pico Ruivo **1862m/6108ft**	P. de las Nieves **1949m/6394ft**	Pico del Teide **3718m/ 12,198ft**	Pico da Vara **1103m/3618ft**

still plays a major role in the lives of village communities. Religious processions and festivals are undoubtedly among the highlights of the year.

POLITICAL SYSTEM

Political structure Political structure The island of Madeira is divided into **eleven municipalities** (concelhos), in turn subdivided into 53 parishes (freguesias). Funchal, the only town of any notable size on Madeira, is the seat of the political leadership, legislative organs and administration. Madeira's governing body consists of a Regional President and a regional government, with political decisions taken by the 55-member Regional Assembly. The neighbouring island of Porto Santo, forming a twelfth parish, enjoys a degree of independence.

Relationship to Portugal Madeira belongs to Portugal. Since the so-called Revolution of the Carnations of 1974, the archipelago has maintained a high level of political autonomy, anchored in the Portuguese constitution and the statute of the Autonomous Region. The sovereignty of Portugal is represented by a minister of the republic, who works together with the region's institutions. Madeira is also seat of the European Council for Environmental Law.

These sweet fruits are popular on Madeira and the world over

Since 1976, the Social Democratic Party (PSD) has continuously provided the members of parliament. In spite of the »social democratic« tag, the PSD is politically right of centre. Most mayors also come from the ranks of the PSD.

Political parties

ECONOMY

An important factor in the development of the economy on Madeira has been the support of the European Union, which pumped considerable funds into the island. The road network has been extended and modernized at great expense. EU aid is also proving effective in agriculture.

European Union

There has been a sharp decline in cattle breeding overall. Pig husbandry has gained somewhat in importance as a consequence of the increasing number of hungry tourists. A visit to the market confirms the rich variety of plant life on Madeira. As crops can be grown all year round and harvested several times a year, the island is completely self-sufficient in the provision of fruit and vegetables and is, moreover, able to export surplus agricultural produce. The only fruit and vegetables imported are brought in to add to the already rich diversity on offer. Of all the agricultural products of Madeira, **Madeira wine** has the longest tradition. The island's volcanic origins furnish the vine with soils low in lime, complemented by

Agriculture

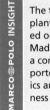

? | MARCO POLO INSIGHT — *Aloe Vera*

The traditional medicinal plant aloe vera is cultivated on a large scale on Madeira. Powdered or as a concentrate, it is exported for use in cosmetics and health and wellness products.

sufficient moisture and plenty of sunshine. The secret of this famous sweet wine lies in the solera refining process, with the addition of brandy and plenty of time for ageing (►MARCO POLO Insight, p. 86). As in northern Portugal, vines in Madeira are grown to head height, leaving the area below free for other agricultural produce, such as sweet potatoes or other vegetables. The second most important produce after wine are potatoes. Bananas are cultivated on the south coast and harvested throughout the year. The smaller, plainer varieties tend to be sweeter, with a more intense flavour than the larger ones. Fish with grilled banana is a speciality of Madeiran cuisine.

Since time immemorial, the agricultural prosperity of Madeira has been hindered by the fact that only a third of the island is cultivable. The small fields on the countless terraces are still largely tilled by hand even now; machinery here is barely practicable. As fewer and fewer people are willing to take on this arduous labour for a paltry financial reward, the economic importance of farming is waning – as it is right across Europe.

Topographical disadvantages

Fishing off the coast of Madeira: hard work and not very profitable

Fishing

Fishing is not of any great significance on Madeira. Again, topography is decisive in this respect: The ocean bed off the coast of Madeira falls away sharply and the deeper waters are sparsely populated by fish. Tuna, mackerel and the black scabbardfish are the most common catch, along with monkfish and redfish. Up until 1981, the village of Caniçal lived from whaling, before international protests put an end to it in all of Portugal.

Industry and crafts

Industry is scarce on Madeira, not least as a result of the topographical conditions, which are not conducive to large production facilities. Some smaller firms are located around Funchal, but they manufacture products almost exclusively for the island itself. Eastern Madeira is home to a small industrial zone outside Caniçal. Embroidery has a long tradition on the island, with tablecloths in countless varieties, ornately decorated napkins, handkerchiefs, blouses and dresses, as well as valuable tapestries that are exported all over the world. For many families on Madeira, embroidery makes an indispensable contribution to the household income. More than 30,000 women are engaged in embroidery today, the majority of them working from home. Camacha is the main hub of the basketry trade. This handicraft has roughly as long a history on Madeira as embroidery. As machinery cannot be used in the weaving process, each item is unique.

TOURISM

The annual influx of well over 800,000 holidaymakers secures close to 7000 jobs in the island's hotels, with an additional 15,000 directly related to tourism. The hotel sector alone accounts for approximately 10% of the region's gross output, concentrated primarily in and around Funchal. Most visitors today, as has always been the case, hail from Great Britain, Germany and the Portuguese mainland.

The most vital sector

By the mid-19th century, Madeira was rapidly becoming a popular holiday destination. The mild climate attracted people with pulmonary ailments or gout, hopeful of curing their condition. They were joined by members of princely or royal courts and the moneyed classes. Ultimately, Madeira was regarded as a decidedly upper-class holiday domicile during the cold and wet winters of central Europe. The first hotels on Madeira, including the distinguished Reid's Palace Hotel, (►MARCO POLO Insight, p. 68), were built in the late 19th century. Arriving by boat was both expensive and time-consuming, but the opening of the airport in 1964 rectified the situation and ensured the continuous development of Madeira tourism. Since then, the number of hotel beds has multiplied to the extent that Madeira now has some 25,000 beds in over 150 hotels and numerous smaller hostels, whilst Porto Santo has around 1500 beds. Madeira is renowned for a high proportion of superior hotels – four-star establishments are in the majority. The regional government is trying to promote individual tourism more heavily than mass tourism. Furthermore, efforts are being made to make the island more interesting to younger holidaymakers and improve its image accordingly. Meanwhile, the congress and conference capacity is being increased, as the expansion of the congress centre in Funchal demonstrates; a glance at the prospectus of one of the larger hotels confirms that many are perfectly equipped to cater for such events. Wellness has again become a focal point in the 21st century: Any hotels offer a wide range of related services.

History

TRANSPORT

The topography of Madeira has been a big challenge in terms of establishing an infrastructure of roads to all corners of the island. Ini-

Pathways and road network

tially, a network of simple cobbled lanes proved the best means of negotiating the precipitous terrain, with gorges traversed by narrow stone bridges. Tight, winding roads connected one settlement to the next. More recently, wider roads have been constructed, primarily through EU funding, in some cases connected by miles-long tunnels. Improvements to the communications network are also visible in the expansion of local transport services. Most, if not all, parts of the island can now be reached relatively comfortably by bus.

Unique means of transport

The typical Madeira pathways and road conditions saw some rather unusual forms of conveyance or transport in the 17th and 18th centuries: not only the more wealthy Madeirans were carried by »rede«, a hammock slung on two poles. Tourists also took advantage of the service, even to ascend Madeira's highest mountain, Pico Ruivo. The palanquin, a board fixed to a wooden or iron frame, was used to carry people and goods of all kinds. The brace of palanquin bearers needed to be strong, sturdy on their feet and have a good head for heights. Finally, the »carro de bois« was a sled pulled by a pair of oxen, invented by an Englishman, Major Buckley, in 1848 and far more comfortable than the alternatives. Members of high society covered their »carros de bois« with cloth to keep out the elements. Relics from a distant bygone age are the basket sleds, once a usual means of transport from Monte down to Funchal. Today they are a successful tourist attraction, demonstrating the ancient form of transport over a shorter distance (▶Monte and ▶ill. p. 7, 40).

Gone are the days when you could be carried around the island in a hammock...

Madeira's international airport is situated approximately 18km/11mi east of Funchal. The first planes landed on Madeira in 1921 – seaplanes in those days, alighting on Funchal Bay. Later, the small NATO airbase on Porto Santo, built in 1960, came into use. Travellers were then ferried to Madeira by boat. Ideas about constructing an airport on Madeira's only high plateau, Paúl da Serra, remained just that, on account of the frequent fog there. The present airport was opened in 1964. High mountains alongside the runway and unpredictable downwinds earned the airport the accolade of being one of Europe's most challenging. For many years, the airstrip was a mere 1800m/2000yd long, hence the nickname of »aircraft carrier«. The runway has subsequently been extended to accommodate the increase in air traffic: Since the summer of 2000, larger planes have been able to land here. One section reaches out into the ocean, built on columns over the water. Pilots now enjoy easier conditions for take-off and landing thanks to the 3000m/3250yd runway and an improved angle of approach. Propeller planes still land at the NATO airfield on Porto Santo.

Air transportation

> **? MARCO POLO INSIGHT**
>
> *Transportation threads*
>
> Madeira's oldest road was built in the 1950s. Originally, the island was laced with a network of paths. People and goods were mostly transported by water. A simple rope lift was built to get down from the steep coastal cliffs. The locals called them »Fios« (threads).

Brief History

The official history of the island begins in 1418, when the two Portuguese explorers Gonçalves Zarco and Vaz Teixeira landed on Porto Santo. The following year, they set foot on the somewhat inaccessible neighbouring island Madeira. There is no conclusive evidence as to who really discovered the archipelago.

CONQUEST AND COLONIZATION

1351	Madeira makes its first appearance on a nautical chart
1419	The first Portuguese land on Madeira
From 1440	Malvasia grapes and sugarcane are grown

The question of who can lay claim to the discovery of Madeira is still open to debate (►MARCO POLO Insight, p. 166). Madeira was officially plotted for the first time on a Florentine nautical chart in 1351. However, the first colonists only settled on the island some 70 years later. It was at that time that the one of the sons of King João I, the Infante **Henry the Navigator** (1394 – 1460), organized voyages of exploration to find a sea route to foreign lands such as India and develop the spice trade. On one such expedition, the Portuguese captains João Gonçalves Zarco and Tristão Vaz Teixeira landed on the neighbouring island, which they named Porto Santo, in 1418, claiming it for the Portuguese Crown. On their return, they reported back to the prince on the existence of a much larger island in the vicinity. In 1419, Henry dispatched the two once again, this time accompanied by the nobleman Bartolomeu Perestrello, who established a base on Porto Santo whilst Zarco and Teixeira took possession of the adjacent, uninhabited island for Portugal, giving it the name »Madeira« (wood), a reference to the dense woodland they found there.

»Wood Island«

Due to their favourable strategic location, Madeira and Porto Santo were earmarked for development as supply stations for Portuguese expedition ships. In 1423, the first colonists settled in the bays of Machico and Câmara de Lobos and set about reclaiming the impenetrable terrain of Madeira by means of fire clearance. Sometimes the fires got out of hand; on one occasion, so the story goes, the settlers were forced to flee to their ships and wait on board for two days until the flames had died down. After seven years, or thereabouts, the virgin forest had been virtually destroyed.

Fire clearance

Wicker basket sleigh rides have a long tradition on Madeira

Agricultural basis

In 1440, Henry the Navigator had the first Malvasia vines brought to Madeira from Crete, and rapid growth of viniculture ensued. **Sugarcane** also thrived, and before long the wood island was renowned throughout Europe for the excellent quality of its sugar. The arduous labour on the sugarcane plantations and in the sugar mills as well as the construction of the terraced fields and irrigation channels (levadas; ▶MARCO POLO Insight, p. 174) was carried out by slaves, initially drawn from the aboriginal people of the Canaries and later from the west coast of Africa.

SPECIAL STATUS IN THE COLONIAL EMPIRE

1497	Funchal is declared capital of the island and Madeira is accorded special status.
16th century	Pirates are attracted by the island's riches.
1580 – 1640	Madeira passes into Spanish hands.

Sugar loaves in the coat of arms

In 1497 King Manuel I annexed the archipelago into his kingdom, declaring Funchal the capital of Madeira. In 1508 Funchal was granted city status, thus earning the right to present its own coat of arms: It depicts five sugar loaves, a reference to Madeira as a major supplier of sugar. In 1514, as the local population approached 5000, Funchal's cathedral was consecrated and a bishop appointed. The diocese of Funchal incorporated all of Portugal's occupied territories in Africa and Asia, all the way to Japan.

Sugar was pressed into sugar loaves using clay cones

The sugarboom on Madeira ended as early as the beginning of the **Madeirans** 16th century, the soil having effectively been drained of its nutrients. **become** Furthermore Europe's biggest supplier of sugar was facing severe **Portuguese** competition from another Portuguese colony, Brazil. Madeira, however, profited from its special status in the Portuguese colonial empire: From 1497 onwards, the island's inhabitants were no longer classed as colonials, but as Portuguese citizens. This allowed them to concentrate on self-sufficient farming unlike their colonial counterparts, who were restricted to monoculture in the interests of profit and were dependent on the motherland for their own needs. As state nationals, the inhabitants of Madeira enjoyed another privilege: All overseas products had to be shipped via Portuguese ports. Instead of manufacturing their own sugar, the Madeirans made money through interim storage and by selling Bra-

> **?** **MARCO POLO INSIGHT**
>
> *Famous sugar merchant*
>
> Between 1479 and 1482, Christopher Columbus is said to have lived on Porto Santo and was married to Filipa Perestrelo, the daughter of the first Portuguese governor. Columbus was involved in the lucrative sugar trade at the time.

zilian sugar. Many owners of large estates switched their attention from sugarcane cultivation to grapevines. Madeira shipped its sought-after wine (▶MARCO POLO Insight, p. 86) to Portugal and its colonies overseas, and later straight to England and the British colonies. In 1643, Portugal's King João IV issued a decree that would prove highly lucrative for Madeira, whereby every ship bound for Brazil first had to stop at Funchal to load foodstuffs. Ships from other seafaring states also docked at Madeira before crossing the Atlantic, taking on board provisions and supplies – and filling the coffers of the islanders.

Wealth attracts predators, and merchant ships repeatedly found **Pirates** themselves attacked by pirates. Buccaneers also attempted to land on the island. In 1513, King Manuel I decreed that the São Lourenço fortress be constructed to protect Funchal, bolstered by an efficient early warning system: As pirates invariably approached from the north or east, they were easier to spot from Porto Santo than from the main island. Stacks of wood which had been piled up in advance for such eventualities were ignited to warn the inhabitants of both islands. But the pirates could not be held off indefinitely. In 1566, French freebooters managed to invade Funchal, their reign of terror lasting for 16 days. By the time help arrived from the Portuguese mainland, all the churches and the supplies of the great trading houses had been plundered. When Portugal surrendered its independence to Spain for sixty years (1580 – 1640), Madeira also came under Spanish rule. Both the island and the mainland were thrust into the conflict between Spain and England and were now plundered and pillaged by English pirates. In 1620, the English buccaneer John Ward launched an attack on Funchal, taking 1200 men, women and children captive and selling them as slaves in Tunisia.

ENGLISH PRESENCE

From 1660	English wine merchants settle
1807 – 1814	English occupation of Madeira
1852 1872	Mildew and phylloxera destroy the vines
1891	Reid's Hotel is opened

The English on Madeira In 1660, Catharine of Braganza, daughter to João IV, married King Charles II of England. The marriage contract secured particular rights for London with regard to Madeira – indeed, the island almost exchanged hands as a dowry. Before long, the first English merchants settled on Madeira. They profited from trade privileges, especially with regard to Madeira wine, which rapidly became the most important export commodity of the island. A commercial treaty signed in 1703, leading to Portugal's dependence on England in the long run, saw Madeira's entire wine production fall under English control.

Napoleonic Wars During the Napoleonic Wars, English troops erected a stronghold on the island against France in 1801. When Napoleon annexed the Portuguese mainland in 1807, England declared its occupation of Madeira complete, but withdrew again in 1814. More than a few of the occupying officers and soldiers left the army and chose to remain on Madeira as merchants.

Economy Mildew ruined a large part of the Madeiran vineyard in 1852; grape phylloxera brought in from America in 1872 proved equally devastating for a large proportion of the crop. It took years for grapes to grow again on more resilient vines. English vintners left the island and many impoverished Madeirans emigrated. Others tried their luck at basketry, whilst new techniques of embroidery introduced by the Englishwoman Elizabeth Phelps led to a small-scale, yet consistent economic upturn. A further source of income, modest at first, was the emergence of tourism in the second half of the 19th century. The now world-famous Reid's Hotel opened its doors for the first time in 1891 (►MARCO

MARCO ◉ POLO INSIGHT

? *Sweet St. Peter's Basilica*

One the sweetest gifts ever to be bestowed upon a pope came from Madeira: To thank Pope Leo X for appointing his son as the first Bishop of Madeira, the governor of the island sent him a replica of the St. Peter's Basilica in Vatican City made entirely of sugar.

Merchant ships in the bay of Funchal in the 19th century

POLO Insight, p. 68); guests included royalty from all over Europe, some already crowned, some not. They valued the healthy, rejuvenating qualities of the temperate climate. In 1751, physicians were saying that the mild climate had a healing effect on tuberculosis patients.

20TH/21ST CENTURY

1914 – 1918	Portugal sides with England
1931	The »hunger revolution« is suppressed
1933	Salazar's dictatorship begins
1964	Madeira's airport is opened
1974	The »Carnation Revolution« brings an end to the dictatorship
1976	Madeira becomes an autonomous region
1986	Portugal joins the EU
2000	Extension of Madeira's airport
2010	42 people killed in devastating storms

Portugal sided with England in the First World War. London enjoined the Portuguese government to seize all German ships anchored in Portuguese ports and hand them over to Great Britain. As a consequence, Germany dispatched submarines to Madeira, sinking the French warship Surprise off the coast of Funchal and opening fire on the town, where a number of buildings were destroyed. The population prayed for an end to the bombardment in a supplicatory procession, vowing to erect a statue of the Virgin Mary when the war ended – and the enemy fire ceased forthwith. The figure of the Virgin

World War I

Mary was mounted above Monte in 1927, financed by donations from all over the world – even the Austrian Empress Zita is said to have contributed.

In 1931, a revolt broke out on Madeira in a reaction to a decree issued by the government in Lisbon, giving mill owners the exclusive right to import flour. This led to a huge increase in the price of bread. Fearing for their livelihood, the islanders instigated the only general strike in the history of Madeira. On 4 April 1931 the »hunger uprising« spilled over into armed revolt, but on 28 April mainland troops arrived in Funchal and the rebels were forced to surrender after brief resistance.

Among the first tourists on Madeira was George Bernard Shaw – taking tango lessons here

Dictatorship From 1932, António de Oliveira Salazar (1889 – 1970) ruled the Portuguese motherland. His dictatorship was underpinned chiefly by the feared secret police PIDE. The constitution of 1933 established his authoritarian form of government, suppressing all opposition. The Second World War left Madeira almost completely unscathed, Portugal remaining neutral. In May 1943, Lisbon severed diplomatic relations with Germany and subsequently allowed the British and Americans to set up military bases on the Azores.

Tourism Regular flights by seaplane from southern England and Lisbon had been scheduled to Funchal since 1947. When the NATO airfield on Porto Santo was declared ready for use in 1960, visitors were able to land there and continue to Madeira by boat. To the east of Funchal, Santa Catarina Airport opened in 1964. This was followed by a double-digit rate of increase in visitor numbers.

Bloodless revolution Following the Salazar dictatorship (until 1968) and the six-year tenure of Salazar's confidant and successor Marcelo Caetano, the Movement of the Armed Forces (MFA) opposition group brought down the dictatorial regime in the largely bloodless **»Carnation Revolution«** in 1974. Amongst the parties formed were the radical FLAMA (Frente de Libertação do Arquipélago da Madeira) and MAIA (Movimento da Autonomia das Ilhas Atlánticas), who sought to achieve total independence from Portugal using tactics such as bomb attacks. Yet shortly before the parliamentary elections in 1976, the islands of the archipelago had been granted considerable self-governing rights as the Autonomous Region of Madeira. In 1978, 65% of the island's electorate voted for Alberto João Cardoso Gonçalves Jardim of the liberal-conservative party, the PSD (Partido Social Democrático), as regional president. The government in Lisbon does supervise the Madeiran parliament and its government, but as far as internal affairs are concerned, Madeira retains a degree of independence, in financial policy, taxes and customs duties, for instance.

Portugal became a member of the EU, formerly the EC, in 1986. The formation of the single European market in 1993 led to Madeira receiving EU funds, particularly for the improvement of the island's road network and the development of tourism. Since 2000, Santa Catarina Airport has benefited from an extended runway, built on concrete columns in the ocean. This enables wide-bodied aircraft to land on Madeira.

EU funding

In February 2010, Madeira was struck by violent storms; more than one hundred people were injured in the floods and landslides, 42 were killed, countless became homeless. Mainly Funchal and the surrounding areas were affected. Angry voices warned that the island's soils had been cemented over as a result of massive development, the rivers diverted in the course of road construction and buildings and streets built on flood-prone river banks, all of which had worsened the catastrophe. In November 2012, extreme rainfall caused landslides and floods in the Santana area. The streets were impassable, cars were swept away and homes were destroyed.

Catastrophic storms

In Oktober 2011, Alberto João Jardim was re-elected as the president of the autonomous region for the tenth time – despite Madeira's previous downgrade by the international credit rating agencies, despite the island's high debts, despite a deficit of several billion that had not been made public for years, despite allegations of corruption and a track record of clientelism. He only received 48% of the votes, which was his worst election result in 33 years. So far the right-wing populist politician has been able to avert the Lisabon's restructuring programme.

Re-election of the President

Arts and Culture

Culture in the Middle of the Atlantic

The island's cultural offerings are not exactly high-profile, but it has many interesting facets. For example, what does sugar have to do with art, and how did Flemish masterpieces of the 15th and 16th centuries end up in Madeira, of all places? One the one hand, the island harbours artefacts of Portuguese cultural heritage and, on the other, typical Madeiran-style arts and crafts.

ART HISTORY

As the economy and culture of Portugal blossomed under King Manuel I (1495–1521), Portuguese architecture found itself similarly inspired. The Manueline style was comparable in creative terms to the late Gothic and early Renaissance styles prevalent in Europe around the same time, yet possessed a distinct sense of originality and clear signs of Oriental or Indian influence too. The ascent of Portugal to the position of the world's leading naval power was also reflected in the nation's works of art and architecture. A notable characteristic of Manueline style is its fondness for decorative detail – not unlike the Plateresque style in Spain – often featuring naturalistic **elements taken from marine life and seafaring**, such as knotted rope, coiled hawsers, mussels or coral. One fine example of this rich ornamentation can be admired in a Manueline window in the Quinta das Cruzes garden in Funchal. Another, somewhat less ostentatious, is a small doorway arch at the Old Customs House (▶p. 51 and Sights from A to Z, Funchal). Madeira cannot lay claim to anything in the Manueline style quite as grand as the Mosteiro dos Jerónimos at Belém on the Portuguese mainland. The island's provincial status and its distant location were hardly a tempting platform for ambitious architects or artists.

Manueline style

In contrast to the Portuguese mainland, architects on Madeira frequently adopted elements of the Mudéjar style. Mudéjars were Arabic artists and artisans who lived in Portugal, reconquered by the Christians, from the 13th to the 15th century. Some church ceilings on Madeira were built in the Mudéjar style. A beautiful example of this

Mudéjar style

This azulejo fountain is one of the most beautiful of its kind on Madeira

work can be seen in the Funchal Cathedral, whilst some smaller village churches also feature Mudéjar ceilings.

Baroque The 18th century saw many churches, hitherto fashioned in Manueline or Mudéjar style, decorated in Baroque splendour. There are countless examples of late Baroque, first and foremost altars adorned with gilded wood carvings in Talha Dourada style typical of Portugal. Where late Baroque meets earlier design, the interplay between the styles can be fascinating (as in the cathedral of Funchal, for example).

Painting Whilst a relatively independent school of painting developed on the Portuguese mainland between the 15th and 18th centuries, painters born or living on Madeira drew their inspiration from the motherland, as evident primarily in the field of religious painting. No Madeiran artist enjoyed a reputation to rival such important Portuguese painters as Vasco Fernandes (known as Grão Vasco), Gregório Lopes or Cristóvão de Figueiredo. The prevalence of Flemish paintings in the churches and museums of Madeira can be traced back to the direct trading relations between Madeira and Flanders, which were in place from around 1472. Sugar from the island was such a prized commodity that some Madeiran merchants accepted paintings by famous artists in return.

> **?** **MARCO POLO INSIGHT**
>
> *Azulejos*
>
> Azulejo, so typical of the Iberian area, derived its name from the Arabic word »az-zuleycha«, which means »mosaic stone« or »little polished stone«.

Architecture in the 20th century In the 1970s, two works by the Brazilian architect Oscar Niemeyer were constructed on Madeira – a casino and, adjacent, a large hotel building. Niemeyer had found international fame on the strength of his designs for Brasília, the capital of Brazil, which was completely rebuilt in the latter half of the 1950s.

Azulejos Azulejos are ceramic tiles, imported from Spain since the beginning of the 16th century. The first imports were relief tiles crafted by Moorish artisans employing reds, greens, browns and blues in geometric patterns. At the end of the 16th century, azulejo manufactories were established in Portugal itself, where different motifs were created. Moreover, they no longer manufactured reliefs, but flat tiles made in majolica technique inspired by Italo-Flemish design. The fired terracotta tile was coated in a white tin-glaze and decorated with metal oxide paint. The azulejos made their way from the Portuguese mainland to the colonies and overseas territories. Azulejo pro-

Manueline style arched doorway of the Old Custom House in Funchal

Many squares and footpaths on Madeira are artfully covered with pavement mosaics

duction reached a peak in the 17th century. Characteristic for this period are carpet compositions (tapetes) in blue, white and yellow with a wide variety of images. Such »carpets« covered every architectural space imaginable – churches, altars, stairwells, fountains, benches, façades and the inside walls of elegant houses. They were also used as street signs. When the royal Portuguese court relocated to Brazil at the beginning of the 19th century and the mainland was rocked by civil war, azulejo manufacture wound down almost completely, recovering only around the mid-19th century. As in Brazil, tiles henceforth covered façades and the rooms in residential and public buildings. Azulejo decoration experienced a resurgence at the turn of the 19th century and again at the end of the 20th century, with modern designs seen adorning numerous walls. Funchal's Museu Frederico de Freitas offers a valuable insight into the art form and its manifestations. Most of the azulejos now visible on Madeira are more recent, commonly mass-produced, examples. They are nevertheless most attractive to look at. Some of the island's churches still feature remarkable azulejo pictures of more historic origin. Almost unknown on the Portuguese mainland, Madeira is notably home to a number of **tiled church steeples**. The tiles on the steeple of Funchal Cathedral date back to the 16th century, making them some of the oldest azulejos on Madeira.

As on the Portuguese mainland, many pavements and squares on Madeira are also laid with mosaic stones in imaginative arrangements. The black and white patterns feature artistic motifs such as sailing ships or coats of arms. Funchal's Town Hall Square is completely paved with mosaic stones in a wave-like form. Pathways of dark basalt stone, a feature of the Canary Islands, can also be found on Madeira; the stones vary in shape and size and are arranged in geometric patterns.

Pavement mosaics

»Remates de tecto« is the name given to the figures perched on rooftop corners, mostly seen on houses in the countryside. Doves are the most prevalent creatures, although a human face or a dog may also be spotted. The fired clay figures, made in the same way as the roofing tiles, are designed to protect those living under the roof by warding off evil spirits.

Roof figures

COSTUMES, DANCE AND MUSIC

The costumes worn by Madeirans in years gone by have virtually disappeared from daily life, reappearing only on festive occasions. The women wear knee-length pleated skirts in colourful stripes, a white blouse and decoratively knitted waistcoat under a kind of cape. The attire of the basket tobogganists of Monte consists of a straw hat with a black hatband, wide white trousers and shirt. Some elements of traditional dress can still be seen, usually in rural areas, such as hats of sheep's wool (»barrete de lã«). Goatskin boots with turned-down bootlegs (»botas«) and white or brown suits, worn with a red sash around the waist, are also a typical sight on festive occasions or holidays.

Traditional costumes

Many dances present a stylized version of traditional agricultural labours. Religious celebrations, often spilling over into lively secular folk festivities, are a marvellous opportunity to see an array of traditional dances. The annual folklore festival in Santana, rich in authentic song and dance performance, is especially recommended.

Dances

Madeira's music is largely aligned with that of the Portuguese mainland. Scant evidence has survived of influence from other cultures, from slaves deported to the island, for instance. A video shown in the Museu Etnográfico in Ribeira Brava has captured singing with such a history.

Music

Perhaps the most typical form of folk music on Madeira is the so-called »desfaio«; no village fete is complete without it. Two singers relate the events of village and family life in rhyme, with little mishaps a source of great hilarity. Instrumental accompaniment comes courtesy of the guitar-like »braguinha«, for example. Other folklore instruments commonly heard include the accordion, guitar, violin, flute, drums and a ratchet (»reque-reque«), which probably originated in Africa. The »brinquinho« is a form of Turkish crescent. Its mechanism features miniature dolls, fastened to a wooden pole, its clappers and little bells creating a rhythm in much the same way as castanets. Brinquinhos can be purchased in many souvenir shops. One very characteristic form of Portuguese music is **fado**. Fado concerts are staged on Madeira, but primarily with tourists in mind. The roots of fado are thought to lie in African or Brazilian folk music. A fado singer (fadista) is always accompanied by two guitars – a regular guitar and a similar-sounding »guitarra portuguesa«. The songs generally have a narrative quality and are often melancholy in character.

HANDICRAFTS

Embroidery – Made in Madeira
Embroidery on the island can be traced back to the 16th century or thereabouts: Madeiran womenfolk were already highly acclaimed for their creative dexterity by this time. Until the mid-19th century, their efforts were almost exclusively for their own homes. In 1850, however, the foundations were laid for embroidery on an industrial scale: Thanks to Elizabeth (»Bella«) Phelps, a dynamic member of an English wine merchant family, these exquisite works of artisanship made their way overseas, to England for example, where they caused a stir at the 1851 Great Exhibition in London. On the initiative of Elizabeth Phelps, numerous Madeiran families whose vineyards had been destroyed by mildew were able to build up a new livelihood. The golden age of embroidery –white work in particular– arrived in the early 20th century. The 1930s saw industrial needlework production step up. The earliest documented record of Madeiran tapestries dates back to the year 1780. Various foreigners also got involved in the needlepoint trade. Portraits, fantastic landscapes and paintings by the old masters are the most popular motifs.

> MARCO POLO TIP
>
> *Madeiran embroidery at its best*
>
> **Insider Tip**
>
> The Instituto do Vinho, do Bordado e do Artesanato da Madeira is not only responsible for awarding quality seals for Madeira embroidery but also has on display, in several rooms, examples of the beautiful handcrafted work, mainly from the 19th century (opening hours: Mon – Fri from 10 am – 12.30 pm and 2 pm – 5.30 pm).

The basket weavers of Camacha
The basket weavers of Madeira enjoy an excellent reputation, especially those in the small village of Camacha. Their raw material grows best of all in the damp valleys of the north coast. Basket-weaving is roughly as old as traditional embroidery. Twigs of osier, a cross be-

Azulejo picture on the façade of a house on Avenida Arriaga in
Funchal depicts Madeiran embroiderers in their rural environment

tween Salix alba and Salix fragilis, are used in weaving. Once they
have been gathered, the twigs are stripped and boiled in large tubs,
giving them their typical brown hue. Basket-weaving prospered after
1945 as demand for wicker furniture and goods rose across Europe.
Manufacturing costs rose dramatically in the 1970s, leading to a
slump and stagnating revenue, but the latter part of the 20th century
saw a renewed boom, principally due to an increase in visitors. Under
the direction of the state institute for handicrafts, traditional weaving
techniques have been revived and modern methods introduced for
the gathering and treatment of osier rods. The local basket-weaving
trade faces stiff competition from the cheaper markets of Eastern Europe and Asia. Unlike embroidery, there is no official seal of quality
for basket-weaving, at least not yet.

Famous People

JOHN BLANDY (1783 – 1855)

Born in Dorchester (England), John Blandy set foot on Madeira for the first time in 1807, as quartermaster of the British garrison. He liked the place so much that he settled here – having quit military service – four years later. Blandy acquired the house at Rua de São Francisco 8, where he founded his trading company, having immediate success with Madeira wine. »Blandy's Madeira Wine Company« developed into a trading house renowned throughout the whole of Europe, with thriving branches not only in England, but also in Lisbon and, later, on Gran Canaria. The foundation of Blandy's subsequent riches lay in his simple and astute practice of using incoming ships that carried coal or other cargo to Madeira as a means of shipping wine at favourable freight prices back to their home ports. Despite suffering a series of setbacks whilst at the helm, John Blandy's son Charles Ridpath (1812–1879) nevertheless managed to expand the company founded by his father. Looking beyond the wine trade, he began to import all kinds of goods, which his ships carried from England to Madeira. Charles Ridpath's own sons, for their part, made a name for themselves by instigating a public drinking water network in Funchal. Moreover, they published Madeira's first newspaper, the Diário de Notícias, which still exists today. In 1936 the Blandy family took over the prestigious Reid's Hotel, eventually selling it in the summer of 1996 to an international hotel chain. The Blandy family tomb can be found in the British cemetery in Funchal.

Wine merchant

WINSTON CHURCHILL (1874 – 1965)

Of the many famous people attracted to Madeira by its mild climate and lush vegetation, Winston Churchill stands out. Son to the Conservative politician Lord Randolph Churchill, he was born on 30 November, 1874 in Blenheim Palace. Churchill first came to notice as a correspondent in the Boer War and stopped on Madeira more than once while on his way to South Africa. The island inspired him to write a short story, Mr. Keegan's Elopement, set in the British community on Madeira at the end of the 19th century. Some 50 years later, in January 1950, Churchill returned to the island. Although his plan was to take a quiet holiday to recover from bad health without publicity and to prepare for the rigours of an expected election campaign, news of his arrival got out, and cheering crowds were waiting when he disembarked in Funchal and headed to Reid's Palace Hotel, accompanied by his wife Clementine, his daughter Diana, two secretaries and two Special Branch detectives. He fell in love with the fish-

British politician

Born on Madeira: football star Cristiano Ronaldo

ing village of Câmara de Lobos, where a small panoramic terrace now reminds visitors of the spot where he painted the colourful scenes before him. When prime minister Attlee called elections earlier than expected, the Churchills were forced to cut short their stay on Madeira after just eleven days.

ELISABETH I (1837 – 1898)

Elisabeth I was born on 24 December 1837 in Munich, the second daughter of Duke Maximilian Joseph. Her marriage to Emperor Franz Joseph I in 1854 was motivated by political expediency, as she became Empress of Austria and, two years later, Queen of Hungary. She bore Crown Prince Rudolph as well as three daughters – Sophie, Gisela and Marie Valerie. Elisabeth I, known affectionately to the people as »Sissi«, was exceedingly well-educated, fluent in several languages, had a keen interest in music and sport, yet was quite probably a manic-depressive. Never at ease with the strict etiquette of courtly life, she drifted further and further into psychological isolation, an outsider at the imperial court. Restless journeys increasingly characterized her life. One of them brought her to Madeira in 1860. She was in poor health when she arrived, and some doctors even suspected consumption. For close to six months, she resided in the Quinta das Angústias, where today, the official residence of the regional government, Quinta Vigia, now stands. The Atlantic island's temperate climate improved her state of health, but her inner disquiet persisted. She left Madeira on 28 April 1861, ultimately returning to the imperial court in Vienna. On 10 September 1898, Elisabeth I was murdered in Geneva by the Italian anarchist Luigi Luccheni. Her life gave rise to numerous romantic novels and many films besides, which generally overlooked her intelligence and education to focus on her beauty, with which she herself was obsessed. Playing the lead in the »Sissi films« made a worldwide star of Romy Schneider.

Empress of Austria and Queen of Hungary

HENRY THE NAVIGATOR (1394 – 1460)

Although Henry (Portuguese: Henrique), the third son of the Portuguese King João I, never set sail on any lengthy seafaring expedition, history would bestow the title of »the Navigator« upon him (in Portuguese: o Navegador). Born on 4 March 1394, the young Infante, as Portuguese and Spanish princes were known, owed his fame to the conquest of Ceuta in the year 1415. As a mark of his appreciation, the king made him Duke of Viseu and handed him control of the defences and administration of the conquered town in North Africa. Old nautical charts, manuscripts and stories told by returning mari-

Discoverer

ners awakened the young prince's interest in seafaring. Appointed Grand Master of the Order of Christ in 1418, the financial riches of this successor of the dissolved Knights Templar were now at his disposal. This enabled him to convert his seafaring dreams into reality. At the southwestern tip of Portugal, in Sagres, he founded a kind of research centre, where the newest discoveries in navigation, astronomy and the like were exchanged and examined in depth. In addition, a completely new type of ship was constructed, the caravel. In terms of manoeuvrability and seaworthiness, it was far superior to any sailing ships seen thus far. Over the next few years, Henry financed one voyage of discovery after another, first the one to the Madeira archipelago, which colonized by 1423. In 1433, Henry was granted tenure of the archipelago by King Duarte. Next in his sights were the Azores. Thereafter, Henry the Navigator's ships forayed further along the African coastline (the so-called Pepper Coast), reaching Cap Verde, Gambia and finally Guinea. The expeditions were not driven by the attraction of trading in gold, spices and slaves alone: This was very much a campaign against Islam. Henry the Navigator laid the foundations for Portugal's development as a colonial power. He died in Sagres on 13 November 1460.

KARL I (1888 – 1922)

Emperor of Austria and King of Hungary

Karl I, a great-nephew of Emperor Franz Joseph I, was born on 17 August 1887 in Persenbeug (Lower Austria). As his uncle Franz Ferdinand, the heir to the throne, was assassinated on 28 June 1914 in Sarajevo, he succeeded Franz Joseph as Emperor of Austria and King of Hungary on 21 December 1916. His unfortunate reign lasted just two years, marking the end of the era of the Habsburg dynasty and coinciding with the end of the First World War; inside Austria, he fell short of effecting any meaningful reforms. Not least through the pressure of the Russian Revolution of 1917, he renounced participation in government in Austria and Hungary, without officially abdicating. Having twice failed to reclaim the throne in Hungary, he was exiled to Madeira and died here, the last Habsburg emperor, of respiratory failure on 1 April 1922. The sarcophagus containing the mortal remains of Karl I has remained on the island to this day in Monte, in the Church of Our Lady of Monte (Nossa Senhora do Monte). His beatification took place in 2004.

CHRISTOPHER COLUMBUS (1451–1506)

Christopher Columbus is thought to have been born in Genoa. Aged 25, he came to Lisbon and soon became interested in the western sea route to India, which had been talked about in ancient times. His idea of launching an expedition to explore this seaway fell on deaf ears at the royal court of Portugal, so Columbus initially turned his attention to maritime trade. In 1478, he paid his first visit to Madeira to buy sugar for a Genoese businessman living in Lisbon. Here, he made the acquaintance of Filipa Moniz – daughter of Bartolomeu Perestrelo, the first Portuguese governor of the neighbouring island of Porto Santo – and a year later they married. As a result, Columbus gained access to the higher echelons of Portuguese society, probably living on Porto Santo from 1479 to 1484, which is quite likely where he developed his plans for a western expedition. When the Junta dos Matemáticos in Lisbon conclusively rejected his request for financial support, Columbus headed for Spain. He left the harbour of Palos in 1492 with three ships and landed on the Bahamas island of Guanahaní (known today as San Salvador) three months later. It was not the Indian continent he had expected to find, but the Americas.

Seafarer and explorer

Nevertheless, until his death on 20 May 1506 in Valladolid, Spain, Columbus remained convinced that he had discovered the western sea route to India. Since 1899 his final resting place has been in Seville, although it is not certain that his remains are really contained in the sarcophagus. On Porto Santo, the Casa de Colombo (Columbus House) is today a museum. Columbus is said to have lived here, although there is no firm evidence to substantiate this.

MANUEL I (1469–1521)

King of
Portugal

Visitors to the island of Madeira are offered frequent reminders of the legacy of King Manuel I, not least in the form of the architectural style to which he lent his name. It features Gothic, early Renaissance and Indo-Oriental elements. Manuel was born in 1469 as the youngest son of the Infante Fernando. When the heir to the throne was killed in a riding accident, Manuel was proclaimed king on 27 October 1495 in Alcácer do Sal. Manuel I engineered close relations to Spain through his three marriages. His first queen, in 1497, was Isabella of Asturias, the widow of the Infante Afonso. After her death, he married her sister, Maria of Aragon, who gave birth to the future King João III. Eleanor of Habsburg, although initially intended to be his own son's bride, would be his third and final wife. Under Manuel I's rule, royal power was strengthened at the expense of the nobility, public administration was centralized and tax and customs laws rationalized. More than anything, however, his reign is associated with voyages of discovery, which the monarch patronized primarily out of commercial interest. Vasco da Gama was thus commissioned to follow the sea route to India and Pedro Álvares Cabral set sail for Brazil. Lisbon advanced to the status of Europe's leading trade port, and Manuel was nicknamed »the Fortunate« or »the Great«. The influx of riches was also reflected in its architecture, but Portugal's golden age would not last long: By the time of Manuel I's death in 1521, its zenith had already passed.

WILLIAM REID (1822–1888)

Hotelier

William Reid, the founder of the famous Reid's Hotel, was born in 1822 in Scotland. He was one of twelve children, and his father was an impoverished smallholder. At the age of 14, he hired onto a ship bound for Madeira. There he hoped to

find work, and he also wanted to do something about his poor health condition. First he found work in a German bakery in Funchal, later in the wine trade.

He then discovered a market niche that changed his life: Together with his wife Margret Dewey, he rented furnished manors to foreigners visiting Madeira. Inspired by his success, Reid went on to build his first hotel a few years later. At that time he still needed financial support from the Duke of Edinburgh. Other hotels followed, such as the Santa Clara Hotel and the Miles Carno Hotel in Funchal. His dream however was to build a hotel for the wealthy. Unfortunately, he never got to realize this dream, because he died at the age of 66 in 1888. His sons Willy and Alfred had the pleasure of opening the hotel their father had envisioned, which is still the number one address on Madeira today.

CRISTIANO RONALDO (BORN 1985)

Portugal's currently most famous football player is from Madeira and was born in Funchal in 1985. He was no older than ten when the football world in Portugal was already talking about him. In 1995, the most important football clubs based on Madeira – the Clube Desportivo Nacional as well as the Club Sport Marítimo – both showed an interest in him. At the age of 12, he started training on the youth team with Sporting Lisabon and shortly later moved to the capital's football club, where he at first was regarded as a mere islander, in other words, as provincial, and wasn't taken seriously. Finally in 2002, Ronaldo became a pro football player as a member of Sporting's A team. From 2003 to 2009, he played for Manchester United, and from 2007 to 2008, he received awards as the best football player of the year in England. Christiano, as he's fondly called in Portugal, made his debut with the national team in August 2003. Within nine years, he played in 100 football games for the Portuguese team and scored 37 goals – in the ranking list for football goal scorers, he has surpassed fellow player Figo and comes right after Eusébio. He transferred to Real Madrid in 2009. The Spanish shelled out a record transfer fee of about 93 million euros. Ronaldo scored a record number of goals for Real Madrid. In 2010, he became father to a little boy; however, he continues to remain silent about the mother. Ronaldo models for Armani and has two fashion boutiques, which he and his sister are managing – one of them is in Funchal.

Football star

ENJOY MADEIRA

Try Madeiran food and its traditional drink poncha, hike along the levada trails, check out the beaches and natural lava-rock pools or celebrate New Year's Eve in Funchal. This chapter offers many suggestions on how to have a great holiday on Madeira.

Accommodation

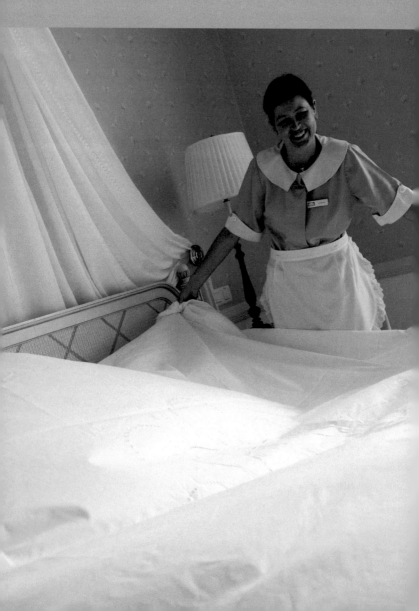

Just Beautiful

Greenery everywhere you look. Nestled in the foothills of the laurel forest is a little house with a pointed roof. The path leading to the house is lined by thickets of African lilies (agapanthus). The triangular shape and the materials used to build the house are reminiscent of the Casas de Colmo, the famous traditional cottages in Santana with their thatched roofs that reach almost down to the ground.

Madeira offers a wide selection of accommodations, from the completely secluded cottages with private gardens and simple interior for up to four guests as described above to bed & breakfast accommodations with native locals (or new islanders) and pensions (pensão), family-owned hotels (residencial, estalagem), to comfortable luxury hotels or guesthouses with spa, beauty and recreational facilities. At the other end of the spectrum are the campsites in Porto Moniz at the mouth of the Ribeira da Janela. The price for pitching a tent is six euros per person/day.

Very simple, very luxurious

The somewhat more unusual accommodations are the so-called »quintas«. Sugar barons and English wine merchants had these elegant summer residences built, which sometimes served as guesthouses back then as well. Christopher Columbus stayed in one of these quintas, as did Empress Elisabeth of Austria and Charles I, the last Emperor of the Austro-Hungarian Empire. To initially make a living, William Reid, the founder of the legendary Reid's Hotel, rented some of these guesthouses to wealthy long-term visitors to the Portuguese Atlantic island. Some of the quintas have been restored over the years and converted into first-class small hotels – or modern extensions have been added to preserve the reception area, salon, dining room and a few suites in the historical buildings. Most of these historical manors are situated on the outskirts of the capital and in the foothill area all the up to the small mountain resort Monte. Some now equipped with modern amenities for the guests' convenience are also located along the mountainsides of Santo da Serra and Jardim da Serra and near Estreito de Câmara de Lobos, Ponta do Sol and Santa Cruz (www.quintas-madeira.com).

Quintas

Advance booking is recommended for the high season (▶When to Go). The price of a double room can vary considerably from season to season, with particularly sharp rises possible around Christmas and New Year's Eve (prices ▶p. 6).

Reservations and prices

Reid's Hotel: everything is done with style, even making the beds

Hotel with a History

Ordinary mortals typically approach all things legendary with a certain degree of awe and respect, which can be uncomfortable at times. But ever since the Reid's hotel – now »Belmont Reid's Palace« – received a subtle facelift, the atmosphere has become somewhat more relaxed: Coat and ties for the gentlemen and cocktail and afternoon dresses or other more formal attire for the ladies are no longer an absolute must.

Though, noble hotels – the Reid's Palace being one of them – usually have porters to separate the wheat from the chaff, so to speak. After all, one does want to preserve one of the last cornerstones of the British Empire.

Very British

From The Times on the breakfast table to **five o'clock tea** with scones fresh from the oven and Earl Grey high above the Atlantic Ocean, everything here is »very British«. And, of course, a **bridge room** is made available to hotel quests as well. A little attention is required, because you just might drive past the fairly inconspicuous driveway to Reid's. The copper sign with the elegant script lettering and the narrow driveway are perhaps a type of British understatement.

A Dream of a Hotel

The founder of the noble hotel, **William Reid**, had worked his way

Soft morning sun on terrace at Reid's

up from a humble existence to the life of a very successful wine merchant. He was also always open to new ideas: Togther with his wife, Margret, he rented out fully staffed quintas to wealthy visitors. After he had acquired a large piece of land, he finally **realized his big dream** of building a luxury hotel in 1887. His architect was George Somers Clarke, who was well-known for his design of the Shephard's Hotel in Cairo. William Reid died one year after the hotel's construction began. In his place, his sons had the pleasure of opening the hotel to the first hotel guests.

Beautiful Luxury

The hotel is quite impressive: 163 **stylish and luxuriously appointed rooms and suites**. The »palace« is situated high on top of a cliff and surrounded by a beautiful park-like area with lush tropical vegetation on over 50,000 square m (12.5 acres). Six different types of passion flowers thrive here as well as several of the tall Washingtonia palm trees, and mighty Kapok trees that date back to the time when this noble hotel was built.

Scones fresh from the oven and Earl Grey at tea time

Illustrious Guestbook

The many famous guests have appreciated the charm of this luxury hotel in the past and they still do today. In the hotel's guestbook you will find names from **the higher ranks of the aristocracy** and other famous people, such as Prince Edward of Great Britain and Empress Zita. **Writers** of world renown, such as George Bernard Shaw, ac-

tors, such as Gregory Peck and Roger Moore, and politicians, such as Winston Churchill, Oskar Lafontaine, Otto Graf Lambsdorff and Richard von Weizsäcker, have stayed at the Reid's at one time or another. But not only celebrities come and go here, so do those with big enough wallets who appreciate the exquisite ambience of the hotel. But, since the Reid's cannot completely ignore the spirit of the times, the dress code has been relaxed a little. And in keeping with the times, a luxurious spa is available to guests in spaces flooded with sunlight, which replaced the former laundry area.

Little Pirates on an Atlantic Adventure

Madeira is not the dream island for a holiday with small children who love to romp around on the beach while parents want to sunbathe. There are a few man-made sand beaches, but they are not exactly right on your doorstep. But there's plenty for little holiday-makers to discover about the ocean, fish and ships.

With eyes and mouths wide open at the amazing sight: The young museum visitors are in awe of the size of the »small« whale exhibited here (▶p. 135). It seems to float, as if moving through water, and is longer than the wooden boats of the men who once set out from Caniçal to hunt whales in the waters around Madeira. Along the coastal mountain peaks, some of the men watched out for the **blowhole sprays,** mostly air expelled by these huge whales, and once sighted, informed the person in command of the whaling operation by radiophone, who then immediately shot a flare into the sky to alert the whaling team. A film about whaling was made right there on Madeira - the early »Moby Dick« hit.

Whaling

Children have an opportunity to experience real sea dwellers both on a restored **fishing cutter** and - up close and in greater variety - behind the large windows of the underground **island aquarium**. From Funchal a replica of **Columbus' sailing ship with pirate crew** sets sail for the open waters, and there is also a ferry that crosses the waters to take you to Porto Santo - the beach and bathing paradise, with nearly 10 km (6.2 miles) of golden sand beaches and shallow coastal waters. On Madeira, a few man-made sand beaches are enticing; alternatively, modern **seawater swimming pools** and a water park are guaranteed to be fun for the whole family (▶p. 72/73).

Ships and boats, ocean and coast

This Atlantic island has many other exciting things to other - not only does the capital city of the island offer all sorts of opportunities for wonderful excursions with interesting destinations, so do almost all of the other regions on the island. In Funchal (▶Funchal), there are special museums, themed attractions related to the history of Madeira, a small zoo and facilities where gravity, the phenomenon of optical illusion and the inside of the human body can be playfully

All around the island

Like once the great navigators: on board the »Santa Maria« setting sail for the open waters explored. Get a sense of what it's like to be inside volcanic caves (▶p. 205), visit an old sugar factory (▶p. 125), enjoy the views from the gondola lift (▶p. 73, 169) or perhaps even let an experienced pilot take you on a tandem paragliding flight (▶p. 103). There are plenty of adventures for young and old. Easy levada trails leading through interesting scenery – across plateaus, through gorges, past waterfalls – are a great experience for children as well.

Attractions for children

Fishing boat tour
Lobosonda, Calheta
tel. 9 68 40 09 80
www.lobosonda.com
Rafael Gomez, who speaks English, offers regular three-hour trips on his boat »Ribeira Brava« during which you will usually be able to watch dolphins – and with a little luck even whales. A trained marine guide and second skipper is also on board from May to September/October.

Aquário da Madeira
Porto Moniz

Rua do Forte S. João Baptista 12 (in the fort)
Daily from 10 am to 6 pm
Tickets: €7 adults and €4 children
Directly off the coast of Madeira, visitors can enjoy the underwater world in the underground viewing tanks at this aquarium. Behind the entrance there are several open pools with a variety of fish, starfish, sea cucumbers and much more; young children can step on the little stairs to get a better look at the exciting waterworld. Visitors get a sense of diving underwater when standing in front of the huge

It's like diving underwater: visiting the Aquário da Madeira

viewing tanks face to face with rays, catsharks and Moray eels.

Columbus' sailing ship
Santa Maria kiosk at the yacht marina in Funchal
tel. 2 91 22 03 27 or
tel. 2 91 22 56 95
www.madeirapirateboat.com
Twice a day (10.30 am and 3 pm) in Câmara de Lobos the virtually true-to-scale replica of the ship with which Columbus sailed to the Americas, the »Santa Maria«, sets sail for Cabo Girão. The crew members are dressed as pirates.

Teleféricos
In addition to the gondola lift between Funchal and Monte, there are several smaller »teleféricos« that run from steep cliffs to a small beach or to a few cottage gardens and fields along the coast – such as at Garajau or Achadas da Cruz (between Ponta do Pargo and Porto Moniz, tel. 2 91 85 29 51), with an elevation gain of about 480m/1,575ft and no supporting towers in between.

BEACHES AND SWIMMING POOLS
Praia de Machico
Machico Bay has been redeveloped and includes a man-made sand beach, a »praia«. Along the Praia de Machico there are a diving centre, several restaurants/bars and lifeguard supervision during the summer months.

Pools in Caniçal
Two seawater pools are available to adults and children; you also have direct access to the ocean.

During the summer months the complex is supervised; there is also a snackbar.

Porto Santo
Sand beaches of several kilometres can only be found on the neighbouring island of Porto Santo. The trip over, either by ferry or propeller aircraft, also make for a fun little adventure.

Aquaparque
Ribeira da Boaventura
Santa Cruz
June – Nov, daily 10 am – 6 pm,
Aug 10 am – 7 pm
aquaparque-stcruz.webnode.pt
Admission: €7 adults, €4.50 children, after 2 pm €5.50 and €4
The water park in Santa Cruz is great fun, especially also for families: two swimming pools (one reserved for children), surrounded by the »Lazy River«, boasts five toboggan rides and four fast water slides – everyone is sure to have fun.

Ready to take off on the fishing cutter tour

Madeirans Love to Celebrate

»É tempo da festa« (It's time to celebrate) – You will hear this all year round on Madeira. There is something to celebrate almost every month: patron saints, a particular fruit, wine, carnival, spring blossom time. There's a »festa« in celebration of just about anything.

The cheerful celebrations are usually accompanied by a **banda** that provides the musical entertainment, plenty of food and drink and often a **call and response style of singing.** The songs are about feelings and problems or conflicts with neighbours or public figures.

Dance to the music and eat and drink away

Religious and traditional events are celebrated differently from town to town on Madeira. Some hotels and restaurants stage regular displays of Madeiran folklore – a show put on especially for tourists. Madeirans are devoutly committed to their religious celebrations, many of which are somewhat like pilgrimages. The streets and town squares are decorated with colourful garlands, and a procession of priests and church followers with a statue of a saint moves through the town – sometimes even at night. The Mother of God or other saints are festively accompanied on boats, such as can be seen during the **boat procession in Caniçal**.

Religious processions

Filled with pride, the locals prepare for the elaborate **carnival** and **Festival of Flowers.** From all corners of the island, locals flock to Funchal every year for the **New Year's Eve fireworks**.

Largest festivals

In addition to the small and large festivals, there are a number of public holidays when most things close down. Some holidays are localized; for example, 21 August is celebrated only in Funchal, elsewhere on the island everyday life goes on as usual. Due to the economic crisis four holidays were cancelled.

Public holidays

Holidays and Festivals

PUBLIC HOLIDAYS
1 January: New Year's Day
February/March: Shrove Tuesday, Ash Wednesday
March/April: Good Friday

25 April: Freedom Day; national holiday to commemorate the Carnation Revolution of 25 April 1974
1 May: Labour Day

Blaze of colours at the Columbus Festival on Porto Santo

10 June: Dia de Portugal or Camões Day; national holiday in remembrance of Portuguese poet Luis de Camões who died on 10 June 1580

1 July: Madeira Day of Discovery

15 August: Assumption of the Virgin

8 December: Feast of the Immaculate Conception

25 December: Christmas

26 December: St. Stephen's Day

FESTIVALS AND EVENTS
FEBRUARY/MARCH
Carnival

For four days in a row, the island's capital is topsy turvy with excitement. It's carnival time. The highlight of the carnival is a huge Samba Parade in Funchal on Saturday and ends on Tuesday with the Trapalhão parade, for which Madeirans dress up in particularly imaginative costumes.

Carnival in Funchal: Sometimes the excitement is a bit much

APRIL/MAY
Festival of Flowers
Two weeks after Easter, the colourful Festa da Flor heralds the beginning of spring on the island. The parade floats covered with beautiful flowers move along the main street in downtown Funchal. Carpets of flowers and flower shows are also part of the programme.

JUNE
Atlantic Festival
This classical music festival attracts famous singers and orchestras from all over the world as well as their colleagues from the island. Concerts are staged in the Palácio de São Lourenço, the Teatro Municipal palaces and in several churches in Funchal as well as in the Casa das Mudas in Calheta. There are also fireworks accompanied by music.

JULY
Funchal Jazz Festival
During a three-day festival in the Parque de Santa Catarina, local as well as international jazz musicians give performances. In addition, workshops and master classes are offered.

24 Horas de Bailar
24 hours of folklore in Santana. Folklore groups from all over Madeira and other countries entertain visitors with their music and dance performances.

Ocean Week
The four-day long Semana do Mar in Porto Moniz offers boat trips, competitions and various other nautical activities.

Festa da Banana
Fruit samples, but also plenty of other culinary specialties of the island are offered on a sunny weekend in Madalena do Mar, where the largest banana plantation of the island is located.

AUGUST
Monte pilgrimage
On 15 August, the day of the Assumption of the Virgin, a spectacular procession takes place, also in honour of the island's patron saint Nossa Senhora do Monte. From all corners of the island pilgrims join the procession up to the church in Monte.

AUGUST/SEPTEMBER
Madeira Wine Festival
Pickers' parade and grape-stomping in Estreito de Câmara de Lobos; light, sound and folklore shows relating to viticulture and wine tasting in Funchal.

SEPTEMBER
Columbus Festival
Vila Baleira on Porto Santo stages events in honour of Christopher Columbus, among them a large parade and theatre performances that recall his arrival on the island.

NOVEMBER
FESTA DA CASTANHA
The Chestnut Festival takes place every year on 1 November in Curral das Freiras.

DECEMBER
NEW YEAR'S EVE
Huge firework display over the harbour of Funchal at midnight.
(▶MARCO POLO Insight, p. 78)

The Turn of The Year on Madeira

Traffic jams everywhere you turn! Chaos has also broken out on the one street that is intended to take you from the highway into the heart of the island's capital. On the last day of the old year, Funchal has become virtually inaccessible – at least to those who arrive late in the evening and are unfamiliar with insider shortcuts. The turn of the year on Madeira is an unforgettable experience – not only in terms of its traffic.

Just like most places in the world, the turn of the year is a public event that is celebrated in a big way – but usually not in one's own town or village but rather in the »metropolis«. Everyone takes off for **Funchal** on 31 December. A long queue of cars works its way down to the harbour, large families climb out of share taxis and busses drop off people who live in remote areas of the island. Everyone is looking to get the best spot to watch the fireworks. The **cruise ships** in the dock are ready. Despite the big hustle and bustle, the atmosphere is cheerfully relaxed. A folding chair is lovingly set up for Grandma; children's excited frolicking is indulgently tolerated; room is kindly made for foreign visitors, who are excited and have their cameras ready to capture pictures and videos of the **passagem de ano**.

Fireworks That Hold a World Record

Then all of a sudden it's time! It's midnight. The first flares are shot into the night. The deep **bellow of the ships' horns** sounds across the dark harbour. Then the most amazing firework display starts. Beautiful colour explosions light up the black of the sky. The sides of the mountains that envelop the bay look like a sparkling amphitheatre. Pyrotechnicians have set fireworks in about 50 different places, such as on the ships, on the docks, along the promenade. One by one they go off. A **magnificent illuminated dome** lies above the bay for a few minutes and music sounds. Brightly glistening cascades leave you in awe, as do garlands, palm trees, circles, spirals and so much more. It's sparkling and glittering in every colour, sometimes just in purple, red or green, and at other times a kaleidoscope of colours fills the night sky. The breathtaking symphony of lights, which lasts about 15 minutes, made it into the Guinness World Records in 2006/2007 for being the **largest fireworks display in the world**. A Guinness World Record technician inspected all of the stations and – only one and a half hours after the new year had started – announced the world record publicly.

Happy New Year!

The crowd in the harbour area gradually dispersed to continue celebrating elsewhere. At home with the family, at a friend's

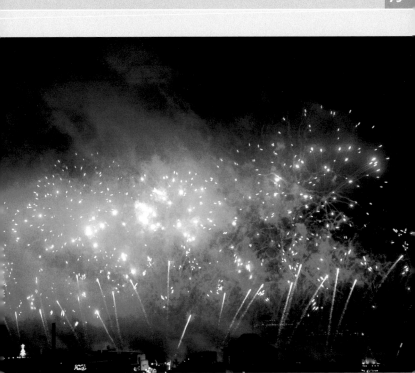

The New Year's Eve fireworks above the bay area in Funchal broke the world record

house, in a restaurant or hotel, everyone is raising their glasses and toasting to a Happy New Year with a cheerful **Feliz Ano Novo**. Some celebrators left home early enough to get a convenient parking spot downtown, for instance at the nearby Parque de Santa Catarina, so that they wouldn't have to walk far to get their **picnic** out of the car and then celebrate with cold chicken, white bread, cheese, tomatoes and of course a bottle of **champanhe**. Life can't get any better than that – except maybe if you're one of the lucky ones who got to spend New Year's Eve on one of the boats, ships or yachts, which are rented especially for this occasion.

Twelve Grapes

Do they serve a dozen grapes per peson with your bottle of champanhe here? **Doze passas sultanas**, a tradition that is still widespread in mainland Portugal, is not very common on Madeira anymore. The grapes symbolize the twelve months of the New Year and are to bring a little luck to each month.

Food and Drink

Simple, Delicious, Down-to-earth

Madeiran cookery is heavily influenced by the Portuguese cuisine,which is characterized by down-to-earth, nutritious fare rather than culinary experimentation. The fundamental concept involved in Madeiran cooking is making the very best out of the island's local farm products, which, incidently, are offered in abundance at the indoor market in Madeira's capital, Funchal.

The indoor market opens at 7 am and is only closed on Sundays. A visit here is a little like being in Mother Nature's paradise. Eyes, nose and palate are treated to a veritable cornucopia of delights. Sweet potatoes, yams, tomatillos, the spiny green pimpinelas (also referred to as chuchu), speckled beans and little red and white turnips all tower in coarsely woven baskets. Mangos, papayas, guavas, bananas, dates, lemons, oranges, anonas, the long cones of the philodendron and dozens of other exotic fruits are stacked in impressive pyramids or artfully arranged as flat reliefs of sorts. Funchal's **Mercado dos Lavradores** is a dazzling experience to visitors, especially to those who love all things culinary. And this goes for the vision of the silvery-blackish glittering stalls on the fish market here as well.

Indoor market in Funchal

Madeira's cookery is, like that of mainland Portugal, mostly traditional, fairly simple and hearty, consisting of local agricultural products and often enriched with herbs. The preparation of foods is not sophisticated; rather, the time-honoured methods of stewing, frying and grilling are preferred, and the portions are ample, at least at the pubs in smaller villages and at home or with friends. A few **ambitious young chefs** are reinterpreting Madeira's culinary tradition, blending it with flavours from other countries, developing imaginative new ways to use the island's products: streusel from the »bolo de mel« on fennel cappuccino; chicken marinated in sugarcane honey for a seasonal salad; »cubos de porco«, a typical Madeiran dish, flavoured with honey produced by Madeira's honey bee farmers.

Tradtional and modern fare

Madeirans normally eat only one hot meal a day, usually around noon. Three-course meals are common, **starting with a soup**; »frango«, »bife« or »porco« (chicken, beef or pork) for the **main course**, sometimes also served with »milho frito«, a type of baked polenta or potatoes, chips (french fries) and vegetables. Fish is not served at home all that often. For **dessert** (sobremesa), Madeirans

How Madeirans take their meals

Restaurant above Ponta do Sol with stunning views

usually have fruit or pudding, on special occasions, cake, especially the spicy »bolo de mel«, a honey cake that keeps for a long time and is made with honey or molasses.

Tradtional and modern fare

Breakfast and a second meal are rather sparse, but Madeirans like to take frequent coffee breaks, usually enjoying an expresso, »bica«; a »garoto«, an espresso with milk served in an espresso cup; a »galão«, similar to café latte served in a glass; a »chinesa« made with half coffee and half milk – the last two mentioned are bigger in size – or a cup of »pingado« with a shot of brandy.

Bars

When ordering something to drink in one of the island's simple bars – such as a »**september coffee**«, a young table wine, whose quality has significantly improved in recent years; a local beer; »cidra«, local apple wine; or »poncha«, the popular frothy drink made of sugarcane rum, lemon juice and honey, which is said to have been invented by fishermen of Câmara de Lobos to warm them up after cold fishing nights – the barman will often serve small dishes of »dentinhos« (literally: little teeth) free of charge. These savory snacks may be anything from a type of beer nut, tremoços (lupini beans) to pig's ear ragout.

GOOD TO KNOW

Breakfast

As in other southern countries, **breakfast** is a fairly simple meal. Only the larger tourist hotels offer a breakfast buffet with sausage, cheese, boiled or fried eggs and fruit. Guests who take breakfast in a café – as Madeirans like to do – can order a »bica« along with buttered toast (torrada), toast with ham and cheese (tosta mista) or a bread roll with cheese (sanduíche de queijo) or ham (sanduíche de fiambre).

Breakfast this elaborate are only served in luxury hotels

Restaurants are generally open from noon until 3 pm and again at 6 pm; dinner is usually served until 10 pm. When **paying**, it is customary for one person to foot the whole bill. Later the bill is split or you take turns paying the bill. Leave a tip, about 5-10 per cent, on the table.

While you are waiting for your meal, **appetizers** such as bread, butter, olives, cheese and paté, which are not free, by the way, are commonly brought to the table. Sometimes even expensive seafood may be brought before your dinner without having been ordered. If sampled, this will also be charged, but it is not a problem to have them take it back right away. Delicious local dishes include »pão caseiro«, also known as »bolo de caco«, a kind of sweet potato bread that is baked to a traditional recipe in a stone oven. In the countryside, these are sold as flat cakes from roadside stalls, ideal fare for any excursion.

Appetizers before you get your meal

MADEIRAN FARE

Tomato soup is a typical Madeiran dish, with the addition of onions and an egg that is added shortly before the soup is served. Another soup is the famous »caldo verde« with finely minced kale, savoy cabbage or chard. The broth can be clear or thick. Traditional Madeiran soups include sopa de trigo (from wheat), açorda (a clear broth with egg, garlic and bread) and sopa de agrumes, a watercress-based soup.

Soups

The Madeirans don't eat all that much pork or beef, but dishes with both can be found on menus in any restaurant. A typical speciality is **espetada da Madeira**, a laurel-twig meat kebab, barbecued over an open fire. Schnitzel (escalope) and steak (bife) prepared in various ways are also served; an example of the latter is a typical Portuguese beefsteak (bife à portuguesa). Grilled chicken (frango assado) is an inexpensive and popular dish.

Meat dishes

Fish dishes of many varieties, along with other sea creatures like »caramujos« (periwinkles), »caracóis« (snails) and »lapas« (limpets) are usually available on Madeira in fresh supply. An absolute Madeiran speciality is »espada preta« or simply »**espada**« (scabbard fish). Some restaurants serve the black, scaleless espada with a **banana**, in keeping with tradition.

Fish

Other fish dishes worthy of mention are »bife de atum« (a piece of tuna) and »bacalhau« (dried cod), customarily served with onions, garlic, olives and potatoes. Further items on the menu include »pargo« (red snapper), »espadarte« (swordfish), »garoupa« (grouper), »dourada« (sea bream). Less frequently on the menu are »bodião«, the bright red wrasse; »cavaco«, a type of lobster; sea snails (caramujos) or »castanhetas«, which are similar to sardines. Those who love fish soups will be pleased with the fish stew »caldeirada« or the »arroz de marisco«, a delectable combination of seafood with rice, a kind of paella, which is however cooked in a closed pot.

Typical Dishes

In Madeira you will find hearty, down-to-earth fare that has only recently become more refined in a few restaurants where the young chefs are open to new taste experiences. Be assured, though, that the traditional dishes of the island are also very interesting and tasty!

Espada com banana: The most difficult task in preparing the black swordfish is removing the dark skin. Usually the fish sellers will do this for their customers. The cleaned espada fillets are lightly breaded, seasoned with lemon juice and garlic and fried in hot oil until golden brown on both sides. Halved (Madeira) bananas, one per fillet, is fried in the same oil the fish was fried in and then placed on top of each fillet.

Lapas: Little effort is required for the preparation of limpets, which are small appetizers. This shellfish, which lives on cliffs and walls in the intertidal zone and whose harvest has been limited, is cleaned and strongly heated in a ribbed cast-iron pan with a little olive oil and lemon juice. Then you »slurp« it straight off the half-shell.

Carne de Vinho e Alhos: A festive stew with pork, which is cut into large chunks and marinated ⬚ first in salt for a day, then for at least three days in a marinade of vinegar, wine, garlic, bay leaves, pepper, thyme and oregano. As an alternative to stewing, the marinated pork is sometimes fried in oil and left to simmer for a short while with vegetables, onions and slices of bread.

Espetada: Madeira's national dish is always offered at every town and village festival. With skilled hands, the freshly slaughtered meat is cut into large chunks of beef right there at the stands. Seasoned with coarse salt and laurel, the chunks are barbecued on laurel skewers – serious espetada lovers decide exactly for how long.

Sopa de Trigo: This hearty wheat soup is best suited for the cooler days. Particularly sumptuous is the one made in Machico and the surrounding areas, where, along with the eponymous grain, also black beans and diced pork is added to the soup. Then, the next day sometime before noon, pumpkin pieces, potatoes, chayotes (called pimpinela on Madeira), sweet potatoes and onions are added and left to simmer.

Bolo de Caco: You will rarely find a festival on Madeira that does not have this round little sweet potato bread. It goes well with the traditional beef skewers. The dough consists of only two ingredients: flour and cooked sweet potatoes. Fresh baker's yeast is however also essential. While still warm, the floured cakes of flat bread are sliced into sandwiches and served with garlic or herb butter.

The Older, the Better

Nowhere else is wine treated the way it is on Madeira. Wine connoisseurs might wonder why if they weren't familiar with the exceptional taste of Madiera's Sercial, Verdelho and Malvasia wines.

Äquator

©BAEDEKER

▶ **A fortunate coincidence**
Originally, Madeira wine had a slightly sour note and took a little getting used to. This, however, changed long ago after seafarers put into harbour at Madeira on the first leg of their expedition and took with them barrels of Madeira's wine; they later gave word that when the barrels of wine were exposed to the tropical heat, the taste of the wine changed for the better, especially after adding a certain amount of brandy to stop the alcoholic fermentation. From then on, the ship always took barrels of wine with them on their voyages around the Portuguese colonies, the so-called »torna viagem«, so that they could enjoy some more of the wine that developed such a unique »distilled«, caramel-like aroma. Later on, the tropical heat was simulated by heating the wine: This process is now fittingly called »maderization«.

▶ **Wine making process**
1 Making of must
2 Fermentation and alcohol fortification
3 Heating
4 Ageing and blending
5 Storage, some more ageing

1 The grape must is pumped into the fermentation tanks, with the addition of sulfur dioxide.

2 The fermentation process for the Sercial takes between five to six days, for the Malvasia (Malmsey) between eight to 2~ hours. Then alcohol is added.

3 **Estufagem process:**
The wine is heated at 45°–5 (113°–131°F) in stainless ste~ tanks for at least three mon~ followed by a resting and cooling period of 90 days.

Canteiro process:
No artificial heating, casks with the young wine are stored under the roof, wher~ they are left to age by the heat of the sun.

Recipes

Madeira sauce

Ingredients:
1–2 shallots
1 tbsp of butter
3 cl Madeira wine
0.2 l brown veal stock
pepper, salt

Preparation: Peel and mince the shallots.
Heat the butter in a pot, and let the shallots
sweat for a few minutes. Deglaze with Madeira
and let sauce reduce to about 1 tablespoon.
Add stock and let cook for several minutes.
Add salt and pepper to taste.

Madeira Flip

Ingredients:
6 cl Madeira wine
2 bar spoons of syrup
1 egg yolk

Preparation:
Shake ingredients with
ice in a cocktail shaker
and strain into a cocktail
glass. Add a little grated
fresh nut meg to taste.

Export today

3.37 million litres of Madeira wine were
produced in 2013. More than 80% were
exported to all parts of the world.

3.37 mil. litres

France
1.022.000 l

United Kingdom
296.000 l

Japan
273.000 l

others
1.591.000 l

▶ Noble varieties

Malmsey: Dessert wine made of
Malvasia grape variety, slightly thick
(high viscosity), velvety and sweet
Bual: Dessert wine, elegant, fragant,
but not as weighty as the
Malmsey
Verdelho:
Aperitif, soft, dry,
smoky finish
Sercial: light, fine
aperitif, very dry

❹ The solera process is used in ageing the wines:
The wine is poured into a set of stacked barrel rows,
each row containing various vintages; wines with
similar character are next to each other in the rows.
The oldest wines are on the bottom row; from these
a certain portion is drawn and topped off with wine
from the barrel in the row directly above. The
process is continued in every row.

❺ A three-year ageing period
results in a light wine.
Vintage Madeira is left to
age in a barrel for 20 years
and at least another two
years in bottles. Bottles of
Madeira wine are stored in
an upright position: It is
already oxidized.

OLIVEIRAS
COLHEITA
BOAL
1984
MADEIRA

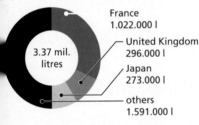

Side dishes The meals are normally served with rice, potatoes or chips (french fries). Other **side dishes** are uncommon in traditional Portuguese cuisine. It is usually worth ordering a salad on the side, which, however, normally arrives without the dressing already on it. Restaurants more accustomed to dealing with tourists are likely to include salad and perhaps vegetables with the main course.

Desserts Dessert lovers should try »leite creme«, a lightly caramelized pudding made from sugar, egg and milk, or »arroz doce«, a rice pudding made with egg and sprinkled with cinnamon. Other desserts frequently seen on the menu are »pudim flan«, a kind of caramel pudding, and »pudim de maracuja« (passion fruit pudding). Common simple desserts are also »bolo« (cakes) and »fruta(s)« (fresh fruit). Madeiran honey cake, »**bolo de mel**«, is a local speciality, also sold as a souvenir item. »Bolo de nata« or »pastel de nata« is a small, round custard tart made with puff pastry.

Fruit is extremely popular on Madeira. The variety of mango cultivated on Madeira (Mangifera indica) is quite small, yellow and fibrous, but tastes wonderful. The **long cones of the philodendron** (Monstera deliciosa), which grow in the wild as well as in gardens and parks, have a delicate, sweet taste when they are fully ripened. Passion fruit or maracuja are used to make juice or eaten as dessert.

ALCOHOLIC AND NON-ALCOHOLIC BEVERAGES

Mineral water Mineral water (água mineral) is widely available, both still and sparkling varieties (com / sem gás).

Beer Beer (cerveja) is a very popular beverage. Bottled beer is ordered as »cerveja«, while draught beer comes in three measures – »imperial« is a small one, »balão« medium and »caneca« large. Imported beers and various Portuguese brews are served on Madeira: Coral, Super Bock and Sagres.

Wine Wine is still the traditional table drink on Madeira; most of the wines, however, come from the Portuguese mainland. A speciality is »**vinho verde**«, a light, acidic wine from northern Portugal, harvested early and only fermented for a short period. Fermentation continues in the bottle so that a fresh, gently sparkling drink is the result.

For centuries **Madeira wine** has ensured the island's fame all over the world. It is drunk as an aperitif or digestif rather than with the meal itself (►MARCO POLO Insight, p. 86). Simpler varieties are used in the kitchen, particularly in the preparation of sauces.

Madeira wine

The most common **grape varieties** are the Sercial, Verdelho, Bual and Malmsey. In just this order, the wines get sweeter and more full-bodied. However, the sweetness of a wine is not determined by the grape variety, but by the amount of liquor that is added and the fermentation period. **Malmsey** is the sweetest and probably the best Madeira wine. Characterized by its dark brown tone, its taste has a slight edge. It is an ideal dessert wine after dinner.

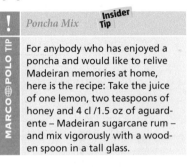

MARCO POLO TIP

Poncha Mix — Insider Tip

For anybody who has enjoyed a poncha and would like to relive Madeiran memories at home, here is the recipe: Take the juice of one lemon, two teaspoons of honey and 4 cl /1.5 oz of aguardente – Madeiran sugarcane rum – and mix vigorously with a wooden spoon in a tall glass.

Bual is relatively light and not quite as sweet as Malmsey, but is also a fine dessert wine. The aroma of **Verdelho** is a little smoky, with a trace of honey. It is drunk both as an aperitif and dessert wine. Grapes used in **Sercial**, the driest, grow on higher ground and are the last to be harvested (in November). The resultant wine is slightly acidic and has a certain lightness, making it the perfect aperitif.

A favourite footnote to an opulent meal is a little glass of »**aguardente**« (literally »fire-water«), a sugarcane rum that is good for the digestion. Aguardente is also an ingredient in »**poncha**«.

Spirits

Popular Souvenirs

Wine and embroidery – these are the wonderful products that first come to mind when you think of Madeira. But Madeira is also known for its flowers and baskets.

Aside from Madeira's famous embroidery and the Madeira wine that tastes a little like port wine, you can also buy white and red table wines at special little shops, mainly in Funchal. Also, meanwhile, the capital city has become strongly driven by fashion, as is apparent when strolling through the Rua Ornelas and surrounding neighbourhoods or through the Avenida Arriaga – where the small old department store Bazar do Povo, the people's bazaar, is located – and the nearby areas. This is where Patrícia Pinto offers colourful, modern fashion creations, as does her colleague Lúcia Sousa, whose fashion design style is more on the romantic side. Football star Cristiano Ronaldo opened a boutique in the heart of the city. The popular shopping malls, originally on the outskirts of Funchal, have now moved to a more central location, such as the trendy Dolce Vita near the Parque Santa Catarina. The smaller shops and shopping centres are gradually being driven out of the area between the harbour and Fortaleza de São Tiago.

The beautiful indoor market in the Mercado dos Lavradores is where the locals not only like to get their fresh fruit, vegetables and fish, but also plants, seeds and bulbs of every kind, from birds of paradise to orchids and protea. Handmade traditional boots are also sold in a small corner of the market.

Shopping in Funchal

At the end of the Cais da Pontinha pier in the harbour of the capital, a souvenir shop offers bolo de mel, passion fruit liqueur, sugarcane rum and other souvenirs, which can also be found in Porto Moniz and other tourist destinations on the island. Very nice souvenirs typical of Madeira are the coarsely knit earflap caps, the jingling johnnies with traditional figurines or jams made of exotic fruits. Madeira now also produces perfume as well as natural cosmetics made of the aloe vera.

Souvenirs

At the Bazar de Vimes in Camacha, shelves and shelves are full of products made of wicker, and they hang from the ceiling, on the stair railings and on the walls. Some of the Vimes basketry is also available in Funchal – among others, at the Mercado dos Lavradores.

Basketry

The beautiful colour of the birds of paradise fills the indoor market in Funchal

Fine Embroidery Made by Hand

There is written evidence that royalties still lay their crowned heads on pillows decorated with delicately embroidered Madeira flowers and that, during dinner table conversations at the White House, politicians delicately dab their mouths with authentic handmade needlework from the Atlantic island. Also documented is the harsh reality of producing authentic Madeira embroidery.

On postcards, stamps and in song lyrics she is still commemorated today. In Funchal, tucked away in a small park, is a monument dedicted to her. In real everyday life on Madeira, however, you only rarely come across a »**Bordadeira**«. These were once women from traditional fishing villages or immigrant settlements who passed their time with embroidery while waiting for the men to return. This was a craft that was passed down from mother to daughter. With the introduction of compulsory education, however, it was against the law for girls under the age of 14 to register as an embroiderer. Today, there are still 3,000 women embroiderers on Madeira, they all **work from home**, have a right to social security benefits and typically contribute to the household budget – even though the amount left over for the women who actually created these exquisite works of artisanship, which were then sold at very high prices, was not very much. But, nonetheless, their wages in 2012 increased by 2.5 per cent.

At the »Factory«

Today, as in the early days of the embroidery industry, agents working on commission sometimes still provide the »Bordadeiras« with new material and pick up the embroidered pieces again for further processing in the **Fábrica de Bordados**. These enterprises are not really what you would imagine a factory to be like, since some of them are still in the beautiful old houses where they had always been. In the factories the embroidered pieces are just washed, ironed, mended and prepared for sale or export. Then the coveted **quality seal** awarded by the Instituto do Vinho, do Bordado e do Artesanato da Madeira (IVBAM) is attached. On another floor, patterns are ready for new pieces.

How Patterns Are Created

Originally, the patterns were labouriously pre-embroidered by hand. It was not until the introduction of the **Máquina de picotar** at the end of the 19th century that the field of embroidery was revolutionized and this arduous step could be eliminated. The machine transferred the patterns via colour pigments directly onto the fabric. The new machine punches tiny

Festive dress with ornate Madeira embroidery

The patterns are painstakingly embroidered by hand

holes through the parchment paper along the embroidery lines so that the pattern can then »drizzle« onto the fabric lying underneath by using a piece of cotton cloth soaked in a mixture of aniline dye, petroleum and wax, the »boneca de algodão«. The **curvimetre** counts the stiches, which determines the cost of the pattern and with that the amount that the embroiderers are **paid**.

Embroidery Secrets

Embroidery has a long tradition on Madeira. Back in the 16th century, Gaspar Frutuoso mentioned in his historical work – interestingly, in the chapter on the psychology of Madeiran women – the creative dexterity of the Madeiran womenfolk who made beautiful patterns of fabric. The nuns in Madeira's monasteries have also always engaged in embroidery. To this day, several distinguished families have their own family pattern, the secret of which is closely guarded; only a few select embroiderers are entrusted with it to use for embroidering.

Embroidery Was Valued

Miss **Elizabeth (»Bella«) Phelps**, daughter of the English wine merchant and headmaster Joseph Phelps in Funchal, taught the children of an **orphanage** in Santana

– where she herself had spent some time, because the climate on the north coast was more advantageous to her health – which was connected to the Santa Clara Covent, the fine English art of embroidery on cotton. She took a few of the embroidered pieces with her on her regular trips to England hoping to raise funds for the convent and the children by trying to sell some pieces. The Phelps family was a well-known missionary family in England, and so, in 1851, Bella received an invitation to the **World Exhibition in London**. The English merchants Frank and Robert Wilkinson became very interested in her beautiful merchandise and, in 1862, they laid the groundwork for the industrialization and export of Madeira embroidery on a larger scale.

Most Valuable Pieces

The traditional **flower basket patterns** carefully stitched white on white by hand have made Madeira embroidery world famous – and inspired many imitations as well. Soon blue and brown yarns were add in embroidery, and the cotton fabric traditionally used in embroidery was complemented by **linen, organdy, batiste and silk**. The embroiderers **still work several thousand hours** on the finest pieces. Meanwhile, constantly new designs are emerging on the market, many of them from foreign designers.

Ups And Downs

Around 1880, the English ladies seemed to have become somewhat bored with the fine works of artisanship from Madeira. Exports were stagnating and even declining a bit at times. In 1891, German merchants proceeded to take over the market. By 1906, six of the eight embroidery businesses on Madeira were under German management. However, during World War I, all of the German properties in Portugal were confiscated – including the embroidery factories on Madeira. In 1916, Americans entered the scene and helped to revitalize the embroidery sector. By 1923, 70,000 jobs on Madeira were directly and indirectly conntected to the embroidery industry.

Control – Competition

In 1937, the »**Grémio**«, an umbrella organization, was founded. The organization implemented a rigorous quality control system, founded **embroidery schools**, established **scales of prices**, made available subsidies for housing and provided for advertising at international trade fairs. A percentage of the sales funded the umbrella organization. In the course of the revolution in 1974, the Grémio was ousted and replaced by a commission. The commission focuses, together with the **Institute for Embroidery and Handicrafts** (now the Instituto do Vinho, do Bordado e do Artesanato da Madeira – IVBAM, which was established in 1978 and later added wine to its programme, on the successful continuation of production – especially since the competition from the Far East has grown and is impacting Madeira's industry more and more.

Experience Nature

Enticing blue ocean and marvelous levada trails, steep peaks and ancient forests, well-maintained golf greens, beaches and rocky shores – there is an abundance of recreational activities for you to enjoy on Madeira.

A HIKER'S HEAVEN

Especially hikers will be thrilled with the many possibilities available to them on Madeira, whether hiking on your own or with a tour guide. Stunning moors and laurel forests, quaint cottage gardens and ancient villages and breathtaking fishermen trails that run along the Atlantic coast: The best way to discover the beauty of the island is on foot. However, frequently trail signage and the condition of the trails leave much to be desired.

Exploring the island on foot

Anyone who visits Madeira should take a hike along one of the levadas (▶MARCO POLO Insight, p. 174), at least once. Even the most well-travelled hikers delight in the unique, primordial nature of the territory, which can be savoured on the simplest of walks. Levada hiking tours are marvellously varied and are an ideal way of getting to know the island's different regions beyond the usual tourist attractions. Labourers originally used the pathways along the levadas, that is to say, they were not created as hiking trails – in common with most Mediterranean countries, Madeira has no hiking tradition to speak of. Hence, the levada trails are rarely marked and are often poor in quality, sometimes leading up steep mountain inclines or cutting into sheer cliff faces. They

Along the levada trails

MARCO POLO TIP

Pretty strenuous   Insider Tip

An old mule trail runs from the Eira do Serrado viewing point to Curral das Freiras. The trail is not difficult, but it can be fairly strenuous: From a height of over 400m/1,300ft, it winds its way down steeply to the road and continues to the centre of the town (round-trip approx. 3 hours).

may also not be completely safe, for example when the uphill trail alongside the water channel disappears, and the only means of progress is a balancing act on the levada wall! A head for heights and sure-footedness are essential. The vagaries of the weather can also bring about rapid changes in the state of the trails. Barriers send out a clear warning: Walkers have fallen to their death on these paths.

You can't miss the highest peaks in the interior of the island

Weather

Before undertaking a hike in the mountains, be sure to take note of the weather forecast and be mindful of any warnings. Sudden changes in the weather can have fatal consequences!

Hiking gear

Since it is easy to become dehydrated, always bring enough water on short and long hikes. While sturdy footwear with grip soles should suffice for shorter walks, you should wear hiking boots and appropriate hiking socks on longer hikes. It is also worth considering useful items such as a rain cape, weatherproof jacket and perhaps hiking poles for a more extensive levada hike. Some levada trails pass through tunnels, so a pocket torch might be an asset. Crossing narrow watercourses can quickly lead to wet feet. Be sure to also throw a hiking guidebook and a trail map into your backpack. Recommended hiking guidebooks are listed under the heading ▶Literature. Books and maps can be purchased in the Madeiran tourist information offices, as well as in bookshops and at kiosks.

Recommended hikes

The tourist information centres usually recommend levada trails that are easy to negotiate under normal circumstances. Exact directions can be found in good hiking guides. It is prudent to have a tourist information office check on the current condition of a particular levada trail, as it may be closed because of weather conditions. Additional walks and hikes are suggested by town under ▶Sights from A

**To many, this is the best way to experience Madeira:
hiking in the laurel forest**

to Z in the red chapter of this travel guide. Those who prefer not to leave anything to chance can take part in one of the many levada hikes led by guides.

BEACHES ON MADEIRA AND PORTO SANTO

Madeira cannot claim to be the greatest island for bathing. Its few beaches are generally pebbly rather than sandy. Bathing shoes or sandals and a padding of sorts under your towel or blanket come in very handy on a pebbly beach. However, there are now also several **bays** in which the pebbly surface gave way to **golden sand beaches** – imported from North Africa. In addition to the **famous lava swimming pools** on Porto Moniz, several new seawater swimming pools have been built along the coast in recent years, and the regular swimming pools have been modernized.

Porto Santo, on the other hand, has sand aplenty: the 9km/5.5mi of beach at Campo de Baixo are popular during the holiday season and on weekends for Madeiran families, but it is still possible to find a quiet spot.

> **MARCO ☉ POLO INSIGHT**
>
> **?** *Sand from the desert*
>
> To create the artificial sand beach in Calheta, no less than 40,000 cubic metres/1.4 million cubic feet of golden desert sand was shipped by container from Morocco.

The only natural **sandy beach** is the »Prainha« beach – literally, the little beach – between Caniçal and the Ponta de São Lourenço peninsula. The sand beaches in Calheta und Machico are man-made. Stony and **pebbly beaches, rough in places**, can be found at **Ribeira Brava** and **Ponta do Sol**, for example. At **Madalena do Mar** there are two places to go swimming, one before and one after the tunnel. **Fajã dos Padres** comprises a handful of houses and a simple restaurant on a pebble beach with concrete flagstones. Access is by boat or the elevator which descends from the top of the Cabo Girão. There are also coarse pebble beaches to the east, in **Santa Cruz**. At the western edge of **Funchal** lies Praia Formosa, its atmosphere somewhat tarnished by the oil tanks close by. In some places, such as **Calheta**, breakwaters divide bathing areas from the open sea, their calmer waters making swimming more manageable. **Faial** boasts an artificial lagoon, offering swimmers protection from the more powerful waves.

Beaches and other bathing areas on Madeira

An excellent alternative comes in the form of naturally occurring **lava swimming pools**. They have the great advantage of offering respite from the full force of incoming waves. Bathing shoes with

Seawater swimming pools

! *The best beaches* **Insider Tip**

- Lava swimming pools in Porto Moniz
- Porto Santo sand beach
- Santa Cruz water park
- Complexo Balnear da Ponta Gorda in Funchal

non-slip soles are recommended. Two particularly charming lava swimming pools can be found in **Porto Moniz**, for instance. The newer of the two is a regular swimming pool with ample space to lie down, plus toilets and restaurant. The other is a lava landscape with sectioned-off pools.

Smaller, artificial pools, into which tidal seawater flows, can be found in **Seixal, Ponta Delgada and Porto da Cruz**. Waves splash into these basins at high tide, while at low tide, the water is more placid and swimming a real pleasure. There is usually a nominal admission charge, which includes the use of changing facilities and toilets. The **Caniço de Baixo** tourism centre has two beautiful seawater swimming pools at Rocamar and Galomar. The sea pools of **Santa Cruz** and **Ribeira Brava** are also frequented by local Madeirans. No less popular are the new Piscinas das Salinas in **Câmara do Lobos** and the bathing complex in Caniçal.

Public swimming pools
Virtually every Funchal hotel has its own swimming pool, and some even have their own small lava pools. There are also several good **public swimming baths** – both with man-made pools and bathing spots in the sea, or seawater basins. East of the Fortaleza de São Tiago lies the Barreirinha complex. The Complexo Balnear do Lido in the hotel zone is currently closed due to storm damage und is in the process of being restored. Further west lie the Clube Naval and the Complexo Balnear das Poças do Governador. The most modern of all is the Complexo Balnear da Ponta Gorda, with several pools and a seawater basin.

WATER SPORTS

Sailing
Sailors can aim for the **Funchal Marina** with some 130 mooring berths, the new marinas of Calheta, Lugar do Baixo, east of Ponta do Sol, and Porto Moniz, as well as the marina of **Porto Santo**. A yacht-master certificate is required to rent a sailing boat. Information can be obtained from tourist offices.

Windsurfing and surfing
Madeira's rocky coastline does not provide ideal conditions for windsurfers. The waves on the north coast are likely to be too violent and the winds on the south coast too weak. Waves and wind are rarely ideal for even skilled surfers either. The beach at Porto Santo is far better territory.

Bathing in the calm sea water of the lava pools is a very pleasurable experience

The Atlantic Ocean around Madeira and Porto Santo offers a whole world of experience for divers. Some companies have specialized in diving expeditions and equipment rental. They offer, for example, dives to wrecked ships, but also into marine protected areas of Madeira's nature park reserve. There are a variety of options available to those who want to learn how to dive, such as diving classes in the Aquário da Madeira in Porto Moniz.

Scuba diving

OTHER RECREATIONAL ACTIVITIES

The island's politicians on Madeira are working very hard to create an image as a prized golf destination. Madeira is home to two outstandingly landscaped golf courses. The slightly older of the two, in **Santo da Serra**, is famous for its location at a height of 670m/2100ft and stunning views. The 27-hole complex was designed by Robert Trent Jones, Sr in 1991. A hilly 18-hole course lies alongside the Quinta do Palheiro above Funchal. Nick Faldo, professional golfer and owner of Faldo Design, is being considered for the golf course design in the western part of Madeira.

Golf

In 2004, **Porto Santo** also built a golf course: With the Spanish champion Severiano Ballesteros acting as a design consultant, an 18-hole course and pitch and putt (under floodlights) were created between Capela de São Pedro and the north coast.

Biking   Biking is gaining in popularity on Madeira. Numerous hotels rent out bicycles. Assistance is available from tourist information office. Madeira's motorists are not necessarily used to the presence of cyclists, but with new roads and tunnels attracting through-traffic, many a (coastal) road can be considered for a bike ride. Whereas the topography of the island is predominantly suited to **proficient or seasoned cyclists**, the more even terrain of **Porto Santo** is easier to negotiate: Almost half of the 10km/6mi-long route commencing at the harbour and following the sandy beach to Calheta consists of a designated cycle track (▶MARCO POLO Tip p. 193).

Mountain biking   Mountain bike tours on Madeira are not for novices. Before taking on any tours, guided or otherwise, a good 1000km/600mi of pedal work should be a minimum requirement. With that, fun and adventure are guaranteed.

Angling, deep sea fishing   **Deep sea fishing** trips – for a full day or half a day – are offered by various agencies at Funchal harbour. Hotels will provide assistance in looking for and confirming bookings. With a little luck, you will get to see dolphins or even whales.

Biking – the right pace for exploring the island

Gorges and waterfalls, such as the upper river runs of the Ribeira do Alecrim or the Ribeiro do Poço do Bezerro, are great for canyoning. One of the canyoning spots of the island is at the Ribeiro Frio (rappel six times; maximum distance 20m/65.6ft). The Ponta de São Lourenço is wonderfully suited for combined hiking/kajaking tours.

Canyoning, kajak

The fearless can jump off the considerable heights of the south coast at Arco da Calheta. Paragliders experience a spectacular flight for 20 to 30 minutes, as they float over the Atlantic and the coast.

Paragliding

If you are interested in seabirds, you will have a field day on Madeira: One-day cruises with a stop at the **Ilhas Desertas** (literally, deserted islands) to explore the islands, which once pirates used as their hideaway, are offered. Boat trips also go to the new **marine protected areas of Madeira's nature park reserve**, which include the Ilhas Desertas, Garajau, Rocha do Navio/Santana and Porto Santo's nature reserve.

Birdwatching

The Madeirans are enthusiastic football fans. The **Estádio dos Barreiros** is located north of the hotel zone on the Rua do Dr Pita. The two football clubs **Marítimo Funchal** and **Nacional Funchal** based in Madeira play on the Portuguese Primeira Liga (Premier League).

Football

Sporting activities offered

GOLF
Palheiro Golf Club
Rua do Balancal 29
São Gonçalo
tel. 2 91 79 21 16
www.palheirogolf.com
Lies high up in the mountains on the property of the quinta with the same name (18 holes, par of 72 course).

Santo da Serra Golf Club
Santo António da Serra
tel. 2 91 55 01 00
www.santodaserragolf.com
The oldest golf course of the island is the Santo da Serra Golf Club; the first holes were built in 1933. The Madeira Islands Open on the PGA European Tour takes place on the newly designed 27-hole golf course of this club.

Porto Santo Golf Course
Sítio da Lapeira de Dentro
Porto Santo
tel. 2 91 98 37 77/8
www.portosantogolfe.com
The Porto Santo golf course built in 2004 is about 6,500m/7,000yds long (18 holes, par of 72 course).

CANYONING
Madeira Adventure Kingdom
Estrada da Eira do Serrado Nº 38B
Santo Antonio, Funchal
tel. 351 968 101 870
Also offers levada walks, scuba diving, whale watching.

Those who dare to jump have a breathtaking view of the coast and Atlantic

BIRDWATCHING
Madeira Wind Birds
Rua da Penha, 10 J
Funchal
tel. 9 17 77 74 41
www.madeirawindbirds.com
http://oceanodroma.com
Catarina Fagundes and Hugo Romero, two local biologists, offer land and sea bird watching trips. Seabirds are observed from a motorized raft.

DIVING
Madeira Divepoint
Hotel Madeira Carlton
Largo António Nobre
Funchal
tel. 2 91 23 95 79
Mobile 9 17 73 63 96
www.madeiradivepoint.com
Wilfried and Ralf offer basic diving courses that take place in the pool. they also offer real dives.

Porto Santo Sub
Clube Naval do Porto Santo
tel. 2 91 98 32 59
Mobile 9 16 03 39 97
www.portosantosub.com
Ricardo and Joana's diving centre is located at the marina in Porto Santo; dives start from here.

MOUNTAIN BIKING
Bike station
Reception desk in the Hotel Royal Orchid (Info/booking)
tel. 2 91 93 46 00
Mobile 9 66 75 47 84
Albano Lopes works with experienced biking guides who know Madeira like their own backyard.

HIKING
Madeira Explorers
Centro Comercial Monumental Lido, 1° Andar, Shop 23
Funchal
tel. 2 91 76 37 01
Mobile 9 69 52 80 22
www.madeira-levada-walks.com
www.madeirawandern.com (blog)
Madeira Explorers offers guided hiking tours along the levada trails, in the mountains and along mountain ridges. The walks are led by certified local guides. All sorts of hikes are available, from easy short hikes to demanding long hikes. Advice on hiking gear is provided, and rental backpacks and hiking poles are available.

TOURS

On these island tours you will see just how diverse Madeira really is. Take in the island's magnificent mountain landscapes, spectacular coastlines, the opulence of the flowering plant world and the friendly little mountain and fishing villages. Discover your favourite place, as once Winston Churchill did.

Tour Overview

The following four tours are not for those in a hurry. Take time to marvel at the splendid natural landscape and to enjoy the island's daily life and hidden treasures.

Tour 1 **Through the Mountains to the Eastern Peninsula**

Lovers of basketry and whales will find much to their taste on this tour. After a bite to eat in Machico, the trail continues to the magnificent easternmost point of the island before returning at a leisurely pace.

▶page 112

Tour 2 **The Heart of the Island – South Coast, North Coast and the Mountains**

Marvellous views in all directions can be enjoyed on this tour: From the Cabo Girão cliffs you look onto the south coast, from the look-out point »As Cabanas« you have views to the north and from the Encumeada Pass in the mountains to the north and south side of the island. Along the way you will pass through delightful coastal villages, lava caves and a famous pilgrimage church.

▶page 114

Tour 3 **Wild North Coast and Rough Mountain Terrain**

A spectacular coastal route, lava swimming pools fashioned by nature, highlands reminiscent of Scotland and a magnificent mountain pass are the highlights of this tour.

▶page 117

Tour 4 **To the West End of the Island and Back Across the Mountains**

Pretty villages and fishing settlements are dotted along the south coast, where the end of the Old World is marked by a lighthouse with a bright red top. The return leg crosses green highlands and a tremendous mountain pass.

▶page 119

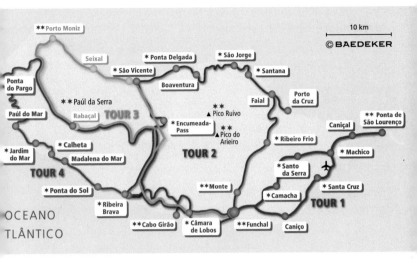

Exploring the Island

North or south coast – that is the question on Madeira. Madeira still has two faces, despite having undergone extensive changes in its infrastructure due to the construction of expressways, bridges and tunnels. The quainter, more densely populated and for tourism better developed **south** stretches from Machico to just behind Calheta and has the highest mountains of the island. The »wilder« **north**, between Ponta do Pargo and the Ponta de São Lourenço, includes the laurel forest region. Most holidaymakers are sure to **seek accommodation** in or around Funchal. The range of hotels here is matched by a varied **cultural life**. Those who relish **rest and relaxation**, waves crashing along a rocky coastline or are particularly looking forward to hiking should take a closer look at what the north coast has to offer.

Madeira's two faces

Narrow beach coves, a bustling metropolis, the highest cliffs in Europe and gorgeous mountain vistas – the southern half of the island has all of this to offer. Since the **climate** is moderate throughout much of the year and the sun casts its warmth across the coastal slopes for a long time, there is almost always a lot of activity on the streets, in the restaurants, on the beaches and even on the peaks of Pico Ruivo and Pico do Arieiro or on the Paul da Serra plateau. The locals are also drawn to the picnic areas, viewpoints and the various

South

shopping and recreational areas, especially on weekends and during the long summer holidays. **New roads** now also interconnect the once more remote villages and towns. The easier **Levada trails** lead past lush cottage gardens. Quaint fishing villages are nestled along the edge of the Atlantic Ocean. The imperial residence Monte; Câmara de Lobos, where Churchill enjoyed painting pictures of the area; Curral das Freiras, once a refuge for nuns situated in a mountain basin; the Encumeada Pass with its amazing views and the Casa das Mudas Arts Centre in Calheta – these are must-see destinations that attract package tour travellers and independent travellers alike. The **bars and restaurants** have adjusted their prices to the regular guests.

The North
To both visitors and locals, the northern part of the island has always had the reputation of being the tough and adventurous companion of the south. The narrow single-lane coastal road that meanders along the high cliffs used to be extremely challenging for car drivers, especially when oncoming full-size buses tried to squeeze by as well. In the meantime, though, this treacherous road situation has been alleviated by adding tunnels built along new routes. The weather in the northern region is **cooler and tends to get more storms**. The mostly undeveloped natural landscape is at this point still sparsely populated. The northern part of the island is perfect for those who love to go on long, frequently quite challenging, **hikes** and for those who prefer swimming in natural bathing pools over sunbathing on pebble or artificial sand beaches as well as for those who do not necessarily need to stay in luxury accommodations. Except for the picturesque village São Vicente and Santana with its famous thatched roof cottages and the theme park as well as Porto Moniz with the natural lava pools and the Aquário da Madeira, there are overall only few tourist attractions in the north.

What is particularly beautiful about this area is the **largely intact, diverse landscape** with its steep terraced fields and the ancient laurel forest, the imposing coastal rock Penha de Águia, where sea eagles nest, and the quaint fishing villages in the small habours, from which sugar cane used to be shipped. The majority of Madeira's vineyards are in the north. The village festivals are still mostly very local events.

Beach holiday
Madeira does not match the common perception of an island as an endless succession of sandy beaches, but the neighbouring island fits the bill. **Porto Santo** has around 9km/5.5mi of sands, offering ample beach space for everybody, even at the height of summer when the Portuguese take their holidays. Madeira, on the other hand, is home to a spectacular rocky coastline with, at best, pebble beaches and natural bathing pools for keen swimmers.

Boat trips can be booked right at Information and Reservations at the Marina Funchal. Half-day sailing trips and shorter trips, for example, on the yacht »Albatroz« (up to 20 people) are offered by the Albatroz Organization. If you go on the »Katherine B.« owned by Captain Peter Bristow, an experienced sport fisherman, you will see dolphins and, with a little luck, even whales. For more information, please contact the tourist information office. An almost full-scale replica of the sailing boat that took Columbus to America was built at a shipyard in Câmara de Lobos. Excursions on this boat, the »Santa Maria de Colombo«, will take you along the south coast of Madeira.

Santa Maria de Colombo: Tickets at the kiosk on the marina or at the landing pier of the former cargo port
tel. 2 91 22 35 65, tel. 2 91 22 03 27, www.madeirapirateboat.com

> **MARCO ⊕ POLO TIP**
>
> *Whale watching* **Insider Tip**
>
> Rafael Gomes takes visitors from the Marina Calheta on regular boating trips, on his lovingly restored fishing cutter »Ribeira Brava«, for a dolphin and whale watching adventure. By the way, Gomes is a committed environmentalist. Mobile 9 68 40 09 80 or 9 14 71 02 59, www.lobosonda.com

To Porto Santo

A ferry runs from Funchal to Porto Santo. The transfer takes about 2 hours.

Funchal: Rua da Praia, tel. 291 210 300
Porto Santo: Vila Baleira, Rua Estévão Alencastre, tel. 291 982 938; ticket price: about €50 round-trip, www.portosantoline.pt

Exploring the island by car or bus

A **hire car** is a good choice if you would like to explore Madeira on your own, especially since numerous expressways and tunnels have been added to the network of roads. The older, sometimes narrow and curvy roads are – insofar as they still exist – the much more scenic routes, but you will need to allow for much more time. **Bus** connections are available to most towns and places on Madeira, but some buses run only once a day. Therefore, exploring the island by bus requires careful planning (▶Transport).

Organized round-trips

Many travel agencies and tour operators in Funchal offer half and full-day island tours with English-speaking tour guides.

Tour suggestions

The following tours begin and end in Funchal, but the routes can be joined at different points along the way and, in most cases, combined with each other. New tunnels and **expressways** have **reduced transit times to most destinations on the island**. It is worth noting that the roads on these itineraries are often narrow and winding, hence the journeys may take some time. Madeira's roads are in good condition, yet often steep, narrow and serpentine. Minor roads are sometimes paved rather than asphalted. The older roads, where feasible, are more suited to the purpose of sightseeing. The most picturesque routes are usually along the older roads. If you have the time, a trip along one of these will be well worth it. If you are starting in Funchal, keep in mind that Madeira has several climate zones; there may be **sudden changes in weather and temperature**. In other words, be sure to pack a raincoat or jacket and a warm sweater.

Tour 1 Through the Mountains to the Eastern Peninsula

Start and finish: Funchal
Length: 1 day
Distance: 80km/50mi

Fantastic views of the mountains and across the ocean are the first impression you get of the diversity of Madeira's landscape. This tour leads through the mountainous eastern region to the impressive landscape of the peninsula in the east and along the coast back to Funchal.

Into the mountains

From ❶ **Funchal, you drive a little ways on the expressway until you reach the Garajau exit and then head north on the new Via Nova Ligação Caniço – Camacha through the Eiras tunnel and the Tunel da Nogueira. The more scenic route is the old airport road that starts in the capital city and then meanders up the hill along the Estrada de Camacha or Street 102, which is still mostly lined by groves and not houses. The main square of the basketry centre in ❷ *Camacha, which is also one of the main stops of many tour buses, offers a beautiful view. The route continues on along the winding 102 through a wooded mountain landscape dotted with such hamlets as Curral Velho and Ribeiro João Gonçalves, whose names tell us a little about the surrounding area (curral = stable; ribeiro = brook). You rarely see people here, and there is very little traffic.

> !   *Things to take along*   **Insider Tip**
>
> **MARCO ⊕ POLO TIP**
>
> This tour is great for taking a few exercise breaks. For shorter walks or longer hikes be sure to take sturdy walking shoes or hiking boots with you, and don't forget your bathing gear!

Favourite destinations

In Achada do Barro go straight until you reach the Portela viewpoint, where an inn, taxis and pedlars await visitors. The narrow 207 branches off to the right towards the popular summer resort of the

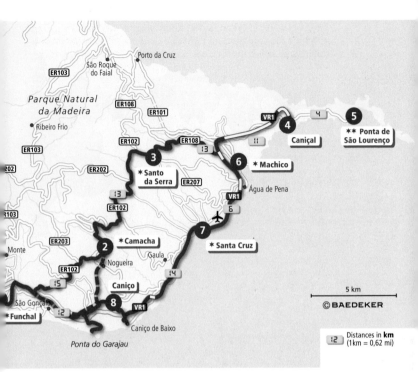

British merchants, especially wine merchants, in the 19th and early 20th century, ❸ ***Santo da Serra**. About eighty years ago, the first golf course was built here on the breezy hills of the island – you have a magnificent view of the island's eastern peninsula from the greens as well as from the terraces of the golf club's restaurant, which is open to the public. Meanwhile long ago, from Miradouro dos Ingleses, the Blandys (►Famous People) surveyed the horizon to the northeast for a sign of their merchant ships. Today, the gardens of their summer residence, Quinta do Santo da Serra, along with the lookout, are open to the public. Even local families enjoy the green space with its small zoo and like to pack a picnic.

It only takes about 20 minutes via the 108 and the Via Rápida (VR) 1 to get to ❹ **Caniçal**, which was once a whaling village. The whale museum tells the story of the skillfulness and fate of these hunted marine mammals, whose natural habitat opens up just beyond the wide bay. Those who would like to do some exploring or get some exercise can park their cars at the Baia de Abra and hike across the

World of whales

bare, rocky ❺ ****Ponta de São Lourenço**, the eastern peninsula, which reaches far out into the sea. Bizarre ochre, rust red, gray, greenish-black rock formations jut out of the turquoise blue of the sea. It's quite a sight to see.

Public beach It's time to treat yourself to a relaxing break on the golden sands of the man-made beach along the pretty seaside town ❻ ***Machico** and to a snack in one of the restaurants in the historic part of the town or along the new promenade of the former fishermen's neighbourhood Banda Além. Finallly, you should also take a look at the parish church of Nossa Senhora da Conceição, the construction of which started in the 15th century when Machico was the seat of the government of the eastern part of the island.

Returning to Past the airport and after a stop in beautiful ❼ ***Santa Cruz** to ad-
Funchal mire the notable 16th-century church, continue on the expressway towards ❽ **Caniço**, where the Caniço de Baixo district on the coast is one of the island's main tourist centres. Ponta da Garajau is well worth another stop. Here, almost outside of Funchal, a monumental statue of Christ erected in the 1920s sits on a cliff – looking towards the vastness of the sea.

Tour 2 The Heart of the Island – South Coast, North Coast and the Mountains

Start and finish: Funchal
Length: 1 day
Distance: 140km/85mi

This brisk one-day itinerary has everything: a lovely drive along the impressive south coast, two lively little coastal towns, magnificent panoramic views from the heights of a pass, lava caves, volcanoes, snug straw huts, the dramatic rock formations of the north coast and a winding route back to the capital.

Beautiful Head west from ❶ ****Funchal** to ❷ ***Câmara de Lobos** just a few
places along miles further on. This small picturesque fishing harbour is situated
the coast below the eastern face of the Cabo Girão cliff, where Winston Chruchill was a guest and painted several charming townscapes. Beyond Câmara de Lobos the coast road 229, which has fantastic views,

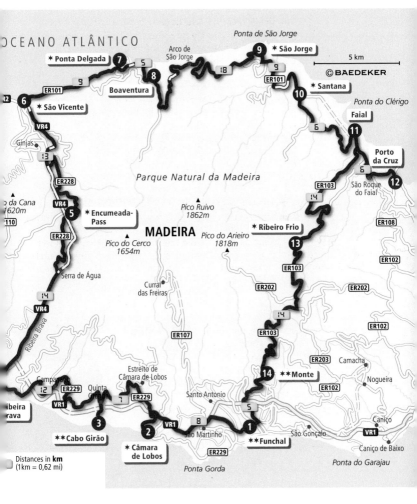

winds its way up and away from the coast to Estreito de Câmara de Lobos, a village renowned for its wine. After approximately 4km/2.5mi, a road branches off to the left, leading to a viewing point at the ❸**Cabo Girão cliff**, a sea cliff rising vertically from the water to a height of 589m/1932ft and forming part of one of the steepest coastlines in Europe. Via the scenic, serpentine coast road 229 you will reach ❹**Ribeira Brava**, a lively little town picturesquely located on the river estuary of the same name (please note: the faster express route VR1 through the tunnel bypasses the town, so keep an eye out for the correct turn-off). The parish church of São Bento, dating back to the 16th century, merits a visit. The pyramidal roof of its tower is tiled blue and white.

Over the pass to the north coast On leaving Ribeira Brava, follow the Via Rápida (VR) 4 north towards São Vicente as it makes its way inland along the Ribeira Brava river and gradually climbs into a superb mountain landscape. At Serra de Água, there is a decision to be made: the fast road or the scenic route? The 228 is by far the more attractive and rewarding alternative, passing through a breathtaking mountainous region, over the ❺*Encumeada Pass** (elevation: 1,007m/3,304ft) and down again to ❻*São Vicente**; the faster route continues along the VR4 through a tunnel approximately 3km/2mi long. Once a simple fishing village, the centre of São Vicente has been spruced up into a popular tourist destination, with lava caves and a Volcanism Centre on the outskirts.

Along the north coast Now take the 101 leading eastwards to ❼*Ponta Delgada**. Ponta Delgada is a charming village nestled on a headland between sugar cane fields, with a pilgrimage church in a lovely spot overlooking the sea and a seawater swimming pool. Beyond the village, the road leaves the coast on a wide curve inland. Just over a mile, it reaches ❽**Boaventura**, both peaceful and pretty; the landscape here is dominated by fruit plantations and willows, the latter mainly for the basketry trade in Camacha. On the 101 past Arco de São Jorge lies the As Cabanas viewpoint, with its celebrated panorama of the north coast. In ❾*São Jorge** it is worth visiting the exceptionally grand Baroque church before continuing just a few miles to ❿*Santana**, famous for its Casas de Colmo, the traditional cottages with thatched that reach almost down to the ground. They are now tourist attractions. During a tour through them, you will be amazed at just how confined the living quarters were for an entire family. The coastal road beyond Santana offers unbroken views of considerable beauty before ⓫**Faial** is reached soon afterwards. Some 150m/490ft above sea level, it is surrounded by wine terraces, sugarcane and vegetable fields. The view from the terrace off the front side of the church is splendid. Next, it is worth venturing southeast to ⓬**Porto da Cruz** with its seawater swimming pool, passing the unusual form of the 594m/1948ft Penha de Águia (Eagle Rock).

Back in Faial, the 103 goes through the island's green interior to *Ribeiro Frio, where the famous trout farm is located. After the tour, you can try some of the fresh trout at Victor's Bar, a popular restaurant for people on outings. Finally, **Monte, just a few miles away from Funchal, merits a longer stop. Because of its good air quality, Monte was already a popular spa town in the 19th century, which is evidenced by the beautiful old villas with their gorgeous gardens and the Jardim Tropical. In the famous pilgrimage church is the sarcophagus of Charles I, the last Emperor of the Austro-Hungarian Empire, who last resided in Monte. From the mountain resort, it's a quick drive back down to the coast in Funchal.

Trout farm and spa town

Wild North Coast and Rough Mountain Terrain

Tour 3

Start and finish: Funchal
Length: 1 day
Distance: 120km/75mi

This tour is dedicated to the scenic beauty of the north coast and the plateau in the west of the island. Hence the fastest route from Funchal to the north coast is recommended. The alternative route to the north coast may be more attractive, but it also takes far longer and is realistic only for early risers.

The quickest way to reach the north coast leads west from ❶**Funchal** through the many tunnels of the VR1, which joins the VR4 at Ribeira Brava. In no time at all, the VR4 arrives – by way of another tunnel – in ❷*São Vicente*.

To São Vicente

From São Vicente, the coast road VR2 goes westwards towards ❸**Seixal** (please note: the tunnel here bypasses the town!). Seixal is known for its Sercial wine – all around the town, you will see the small terraces where the vines are grown. Down on the coast, the Piscinas Naturais, natural rock pools, are wonderful for a refreshing swim in the summer. The trout dishes in the restaurants of this pretty town, which probably got its name from »seixo«, pebble, are worth a stop. The route continues on to Porto Moniz via Ribeira da Janela.

Coastal wine town

❹ **Porto Moniz** is also very popular with the locals. Madeirans themselves like to spend their holidays in this small coastal town. There are a handful of restaurants, making this a nice place to take a longer break. In addition, a visit to the aquarium, which was part

Popular coastal town

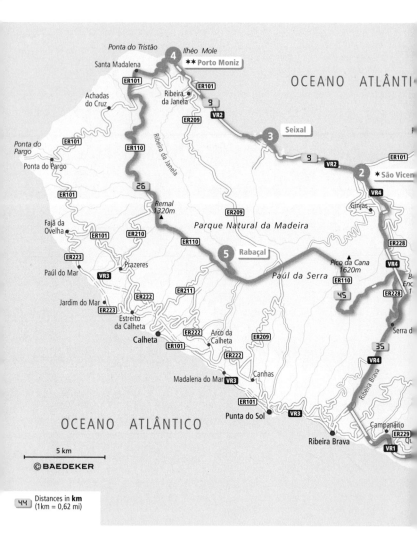

5 km

© BAEDEKER

44 Distances in **km**
(1 km = 0,62 mi)

of an earlier fortification, is recommended. If at all possible, do not pass up the opportunity of bathing in the lava rock pools of Porto Moniz.

Barren
plateau

The 101 then leaves Porto Moniz and winds southwest up the mountainside past terraced fields and some houses. About 2km just over a mile, beyond Santa Madalena turn left onto the 110, which quickly takes you to the Paúl da Serra plateau. The barren vastness of the scenery up there is a bit reminiscent of the Scottish highlands. Sometimes you will see cows grazing right behind the traffic barriers. Weather conditions permitting, the views of the Atlantic Ocean from there are spectacular. At ❺**Rabaçal** you can go on a fairly challenging hike to the 25 Fontes, or you can take a short walk to the Risco waterfall.

On the Encumeada Pass wonderful views of the north and south coast open up. Here, the 110 meets the 228, which leads through fragrant eucalyptus woods and down to Serra de Água. To return to Funchal, take the VR4 to the coast and the VR1, which runs parallel to it.

Over the pass

To the West End of the Island and Back Across the Mountains

Tour 4

Start and finish: Funchal
Length: 1 day – with an early start
Distance: 120km/75mi

This tour passes through various small villages on the south coast en route to Madeira's westernmost point before heading inland across the plateau. Instead of going all the way west, it is possible to turn off early to the Paúl da Serra plateau via the 209, 210 or 211.

From ❶****Funchal** take the 101 coastal road west to r̲MCâmara de Lobos with its picturesque small harbour, where fishing boats bob in the sun, and continue on to ❸ ***Ribeira Brava** (both towns ▶Tour 2).

The next stop is ❹ ***Ponta do Sol**, with its beautiful riverside and lovely church, which was owned by author John Roderigo dos Passos'

Light tourisim

5 km

© BAEDEKER

Distances in **km**
(1 km = 0,62 mi)

family. Over the past few years, Ponta do Sol's economy relied, more or less successfully, on tourism; a lovely modern hotel overlooking the town is evidence of this. West of Ponta do Sol lies charming iMadalena do Mar with its low fishermen's houses. The backdrop of this quaint town is the steep face of the plateau, and on the other side is the wide blue sea.

Sugar cane Follow the 101 coast road to ⑥ **＊Calheta**, once a centre of sugarcane cultivation that now attracts visitors with its artificial sandy beach.

Because of the strong surf, the beach has to be reinforced with huge concrete blocks. The architectural impressive Casa das Mudas Art Centre is located high up on the cliff top. It is a wonderful experience to take in the expansive ocean view while sitting on the terrace of the art centre.

The coastal road now twists and turns upwards to Estreito da Calheta before a side road branches off to ❼ *Jardim do Mar*, which lies on a plateau between the ocean and the steep coastal cliffs and where local surfers congregate on the pebble beaches before taking on the mighty waves. A tunnel leads to aPaúl do Mar, where time seems to have stood still. It is nestled along the edge of the Atlantic and the dizzying heights of the towering cliffs. Take a walk on the breakwater and wait with the locals for the fishermen to return or take a stroll through the little alley next to the rubber tree, which will take you to the new area of the town.

Defined by the rough Atlantic

Behind Paúl do Mar the 223 then leaves the coast, winding its way up to the 101. It is easy to lose count of the bends by the time ❾ **Ponta do Pargo** appears, its lighthouse marking the westernmost point of Madeira. At the church, a little road leads – past the monumental Centro Civico – towards the coast to a teahouse/bistro with beautiful views.

Westernmost point

Further on towards Porto Moniz, the 101 branches off to the 110 after many turns behind the hamlet Achadas da Cruz. This road traverses the barren Paúl da Serra plateau, past a number of wind turbines, past ❿ **Rabaçal** (►Tour 3) and meets the 228 at the Encumeada Pass before descending the valley to Serra de Água. The VR4 and VR1 complete the circuit to Funchal.

Back across the mountains

MARCO ⊕ POLO TIP

At lofty heights   Insider Tip

Ponta do Sol is a good place to stop for snack or some delicious fish at the small restaurant Poente. The restaurant's most prominent feature is its location at the edge of a small cliff right above the beach.

SIGHTS FROM A TO Z

Spectacular landscape, outstanding natural beauty, an attractive capital city and much more to discover on this island of flowers

* Calheta

Altitude: 0 – 230m/754ft
Population: approx. 11,000

C 2

In former times Calheta was the centre of sugar cane cultivation on Madeira. Little evidence remains, with the exception of the Moinho de Açúcar, a dilapidated sugar mill at the beach, and a working distillery which still produces the aguardente spirit and other sugarcane products.

Calheta lies in southwest Madeira, with a good road connection to Funchal, namely the 101. Approaching from Funchal, but avoiding the new tunnel, a **bathing area** greets visitors at the entrance to the parish, with a breakwater keeping out the Atlantic waves to ensure calm waters for swimmers. Two **artificial beaches** were created with imported Moroccan sand. A marina has also been established.

The beach with fine sand was constructed artificially, the jetties keep high waves away

Calheta is verifiably one of the **oldest settlements** on Madeira, receiving its town charter as early as 1502. João Gonçalves Zarco, the man who discovered Madeira, is said to have given large areas of cultivable land to his children here. Calheta later had its own customs post for sugar exports from Madeira. When the fortunes of the Madeiran sugar industry experienced a downturn, Calheta's importance waned.

History

WHAT TO SEE IN CALHETA

Regrettably, the parish church of Calheta is usually closed. The oldest parts were erected as long ago as 1430, and extensive rebuilding took place in 1639, Those lucky enough to find it open will be able to admire the **Mudéjar wooden ceiling** of the chancel, one of the finest examples to have survived on Madeira of this style, which developed in Spain (▶p. 49). Well worth seeing is an ebony and silver tabernacle donated by King Manuel I.

*Parish church

Alongside the church, the old **sugar factory** with equipment and machinery can be visited. At harvest time in April and May, the factory is in operation and its **rum, aguardente and sugar syrup** products can be sampled and purchased in the small tasting room. There is also a small bar.

Sugar factory

Calheta

WHERE TO EAT
Convento das Vinhas €€
Sítio do Convento
tel. 2 91 82 21 64
On the hill towards Estrela. Rustic ambience, great view and specialities like stockfish from the oven, fish soup, picanha (beef) with black bean sauce.

A Poita €€
Lombos
Madalena do Mar
tel. 2 91 97 28 71
This small restaurant a short distance inland from the main road looks a little like a snack bar, but it serves fish dishes that are among the best in the region.

WHERE TO SLEEP
Hotel Calheta Beach €€€
Vila da Calheta
tel. 2 91 72 42 64
www.hotelcalhetabeach.com
Wellness and sports are in focus here.

Atrio €€€
Lombo dos Moinhos Acima
Estreito da Calheta
tel. 2 91 82 04 00
www.atrio-madeira.com
Quiet, nature, 14 individual rooms, generous breakfast and authentic local food for dinner, aroma oil massages in your room and guided hiking tours at no charge – and they speak English.

Sugar mill   The second sugar mill at the beach is nothing more than a ruin, its rusty machines gathered together as a kind of open-air museum.

Centro das Artes – Casa das Mudas   A bit above the town, towards Arco de Calheta, the Centro das Artes – Casa das Mudas balances on a cliff overlooking the Atlantic. The modern building constructed with lava-grey stone is used for exhibitions, concerts and theatres; it also houses an interesting Art déco collection. The building was designed to harmonize with the terraced landscape around it.
❶ Estrada Simão Gonçalves da Câmara 37, Tue – Sun 10am – 6pm, admission: €5

AROUND CALHETA

Madalena do Mar   The little village of Madalena do Mar can lay claim to **historical significance** on the grounds that it was said to have been founded by Vladislaus III of Poland in the year 1457. Official records state that Vladislaus III, King of Poland, was killed in the Battle of Varna in 1444, a crushing defeat at the hands of the Turks. According to legend, however, he survived the carnage and lived on under a different name. His vow to undertake a pilgrimage brought him to Madeira, where João Gonçalves Zarco gave him extensive latifundia, including the place known today as Madalena do Mar. In the dark as to his origins, the locals dubbed him **Henrique Alemão** (Henry the German). He is said to lie buried in the crypt of the small village church of Santa Catarina. Madalena's **swimming area** at the western edge of the village, just before the tunnel, have been given a face lift with new snack bars and a concrete sunbathing zone.

★ Camacha

C 6

Altitude: approx. 715m/2345ft
Population: approx. 7800

Camacha, in the eastern part of Madeira, is renowned as a centre of basketry, hence the procession of bus tours which include it on their island itineraries.

Home of basketry   Many of the inhabitants of this mountain village has some involvement in this craft, which has been a feature of Madeiran life since the 16th century but really came into its own through the efforts of English traders who settled on the island in the 19th century. The bulk of basketware production is arduous, poorly paid home labour.

Camacha

WHERE TO EAT
Abrigo do Pastor €€
tel. 2 91 92 20 60
www.abrigodopastor.com
Popular restaurant in the mountains about 5km/3mi to the north-west on the E 203. Serves mainly hearty food like baby goat stew.

A Cornélia € – €€
Ribeiro Fernando
tel. 2 91 79 28 92
Quail (codornizes) is the speciality of this house on the road from Boa Nova to Camacha. The atmosphere is quite rustic and the walls are decorated with key chains from all over the world.

WHERE TO SLEEP
Estalagem Relógio €€
in the house of Café Relógio
tel. 2 91 92 27 77
www.caferelogio.com
A modern, comfortable inn right in the middle of things; the 24 rooms are furnished and well cared for.

WHAT TO SEE IN CAMACHA

The simple houses on Largo da Achada, the village square at the centre of Camacha, are unremarkable. A commemorative plaque in the centre of the square recalls a football game played on Madeira in 1875 which went down in history as **the first-ever football match in Portugal**. Harry Hinton was the Englishman responsible for beginning the great tradition of Portuguese football.

Centre

The famous Café Relógio, with its unusual clock tower from 1896, is situated on the village square and was once the imposing residence of a British merchant family named Grabham. The clock in the clock tower came from the parish church in Walton, Liverpool. Today it houses the salesrooms of **Madeira's largest exporter of wickerwork**, shipping its products all over the world. Visitors can see how baskets, chairs or complete suites of furniture being weaved. Each piece is made by hand and is unique. Along with various everyday items an entire zoo of wickerwork animals is on display.
There is a **viewing point** alongside Café Relógio, looking towards the south coast and Ilhas Desertas – spoilt somewhat by the road which now runs in front of it.
❶ **Basket shop:** daily 9am – 6pm, workshop only Mon – Sat.

Café Relógio

Insider Tip

On the opposite side of the village square, the Casa do Povo (house of the people) is home to an exhibition on **life in the Camacha region**, mainly featuring basketry.
❶ Casa do Povo da Camacha, Sítio da Igreja, tel. 291 922 118

Casa Etnográfica da Camacha

* Câmara de Lobos

✳ D 5

Altitude: 0 – 205m/672ft
Population: approx. 17,900

One of the most famous visitors to Câmara de Lobos was Winston Churchill, who was so enamoured of the scenery that he painted a number of landscapes.

Bay of wolves
The fishing village of Câmara de Lobos owes its name to the seals (Portuguese: »lobos marinhos« = sea wolves), specifically the monk seals (►MARCO POLO Insight, p. 130) which once populated the bay. Founded by João Gonçalves Zarco as long ago as 1420, it was only upgraded to town and city status in 1996.

Câmara de Lobos is the **focal point of the island's fishing industry**, with the black scabbardfish (►p. 28) in particular being caught at depths of 800m/2600ft and more in the night. Its numbers are decreasing steadily in Madeira's waters. The cat sharks hung up to dry between the boats are imported to preserve the traditional tourist photo motifs.

? MARCO POLO INSIGHT

Scottish summer residence

Hotel Quinta Jardim da Serra was once the summer residence of the British consul Henry Veitch. The Scotsman traded in wine and loved women. He is supposed to have invited them to come visit with a flag in their own personal colour. His final resting place (1857) is in the garden of Quinta Jardim da Serra; his wife placed a monument there in his memory.

Many of the empty houses in town were painted for the sake of tourism.

The vines above the town are some of the finest on the island. The overall impression is of poverty, with social tension as obvious to visitors as to the locals. Câmara de Lobos is renowned for a nicely mixed poncha (►p. 89).

WHAT TO SEE IN CÂMARA DE LOBOS

The friendly **old town**, graced with winding alleys and squares, stretches across a long ridge known as the Ilhéu (small island). Beneath the Ilhéu, a promenade runs along the seafront.

Harbour
There are many colourful fishing boats down in the harbour, still built in traditional fashion at the small wharf. It was here that a replica of the Santa Maria, the ship with which Columbus sailed the seas, was constructed in the late 1990s. It was sailed to the EXPO in Lisbon

In the harbour of Câmara de Lobos stockfish is hung up to dry

and is now a tourist attraction. It is anchored in the harbour of Funchal and is used for cruises (ill. ▶p. 70). The best views of the charming harbour bay can be enjoyed from above the wharf, where Winston Churchill once sat and painted; the spot is marked by a memorial plaque. A new pool complex (Piscinas das Salinas) and attractive promenade were built north-west of the habrour bay. Largo da República has also been redesigned.

Insider Tip

The chapel of Nossa Senhora da Conceição at the harbour is nothing special to look at from the outside. It was constructed in 1702 on the site of the first chapel erected on the island by Zarco. The beautiful altar with richly gilded wood carvings is most impressive.

Capela Nossa Senhora da Conceição

Not far from the harbour, the market hall, though smaller than the one in Funchal, is well worth a look. Insiders meanwhile prefer the market in Estreito de Câmara de Lobos, where many farmers from the area bring their fruit and vegetables to be sold.

Market hall

Higher up in the western part of the old town, on the almost circular Largo da República, stands the parish church of São Sebastião, some

Igreja de São Sebastião

Rescue in Sight? A New Generation of Monk Seal Cubs

In 1419, in a bay of Madeira, the first settlers happened upon thousands of monk seals – »lobos marinhos« in Portuguese. They named this stretch of coast »Câmara do Lobos«. 500 years on, the scene has changed completely.

The monk seal is under threat of extinction, not only on the Madeiran archipelago but the world over. In 1990 the regional government of Madeira took action to save its last ten or so monk seals. And in late 2001, there was good news from the Ilhas Desertas: the birth of **three monk seal babies**, weighing between 15kg and 25kg (33lb to 55lb) and measuring 80–90cm/31–35 inches.

This suggests grounds for optimism that the Madeiran population, now numbering around 30, will indeed survive.

At Great Risk

Altogether, of the around 5000 animals that made up the monk seal population of the Mediterranean and near Atlantic waters just a few decades ago, a mere 300 have survived.

Slaughtered in former times for their **blubber, meat and skin**, which was cured for leather, some seal products had rather dubious uses: sealskin shoes were said to help against gout, the right flipper of a monk seal under the pillow was thought to alleviate insomnia, and a sealskin tent was believed to protect its occupants against lightning strikes. In spite of this, the seal population was never dangerously low – the threat came later, from pollution on the one hand and intensive fishing on the other. Fishermen still see seals as competitors that eat their potential catch and destroy their nets. The seals die in nets intended not for them but for fish, whilst overfishing decimates their own food supply: seals have been found to have died of osteoporosis and undernourishment in the Mediterranean.

The »Monk«

The Mediterranean monk seal is of medium size. It can live for up to 40 years of age and a fully-grown adult can weigh up to 400kg/880lb, measuring up to 3m/10ft.

There are **three explanations for the name**: the upper side of their body is brown, like that of a monk's cowl. The males develop a noticeable layer of blubber around their necks, a real double chin. When they straighten up, the folds of skin resemble the habit of a Franciscan monk. And finally, unlike many other breeds of seal, monk seals do not travel far, preferring to live like eremitic monks in remote, inaccessible places, seeking peace and refuge in caves or grottoes.

Monk seals are an endangered species worldwide

The Human Problem

The monk seal's fatal attachment to its place of origin makes it particularly vulnerable to human interference. **Construction work along the coast** and an **increase in leisure activities in the water** have left monk seals with few undisturbed spots in which to rear their young. Even chance encounters with swimmers, surfers or divers can quickly lead to seals abandoning their offspring, who prove incapable of fending for themselves – another fundamental reason for the dwindling numbers of monk seals.

Protection Zones

In order to protect and develop the existing colony, the regional government of Madeira established a nature reserve on the **Ilhas Desertas** in 1990. A strict watch is kept over the islands, with access restricted to authorized scientists. To prevent monk seals facing a miserable death by getting trapped in nets, all coastal areas have been cleared of old gillnets and new ones are forbidden. For some time now, plans to establish another small monk seal colony on Ponta de São Lourenço have been underway.

Câmara de Lobos

INFORMATION
Largo da República (in the town hall)
tel. 2 91 94 34 70

WHERE TO EAT
As Vides €€ – €€€
Rua da Achada, 17
Estreito de Câmara de Lobos
tel. 2 91 94 53 22
In this historic adega typical local beef
skewers have been served as the house
speciality for 50 years already – variations with chicken and pork have also
been added.

Coral €€
Pr. da Autonomia
Câmara de Lobos, tel. 2 91 09 82 84
Fish in many variations here – as soup
(caldeirada), stew (cataplana) or grilled,
along with it a beautiful view of the cliffs
and the Atlantic.

Restaurante Praia do Vigário €€
Praça da Autonomia – Praia do Vigário
tel. 2 91 62 64 89
Modern restaurant with a purist atmosphere on the new promenade; the large
terrace offers a wonderful view of the
ocean. Local specialities and fish are
served.

Sete Mares € – €€
Largo do Poço, 10
tel. 2 91 94 02 91
Tasteful nautical decor with dark wood;
a few good fish and traditional dishes
are served; meeting place for fans of
high proof drinks in late evenings.

WHERE TO STAY
Estalagem Quinta do Estreito €€€
Rua José Joaquim da Costa
Estreito Câmara de Lobos   *Insider Tip*
tel. 2 91 77 59 36
www.quintadoestreitomadeira.com
Old manor house, located in the mountains above Câmara de Lobos. 44 rooms,
2 suites, restaurant and swimming pool
with a beautiful relaxing zone; shuttle-
bus to Funchal twice a day.

Vila Afonso € – €€
Estrada João Gonçalves Zarco, 574 B
Estreito Câmara de Lobos
tel. 2 91 91 15 10
www.vilaafonso.com
5 rooms, 2 bungalows with apartments
17th cent. country house on land with
vineyards, banana plants, a beautiful
garden and a small pool.

elements of which date back to around 1430, making it one of the
oldest chapels on the island. It was remodelled in Baroque style in the
18th century and decorated with splendid wood carvings, some in
gold. Its walls are adorned with artistic azulejo pictures.

Museu de Imprensa The modern, architecturally interesting and tastefully designed Museu de Imprensa Madeira has an exhibit on the history of printing,
which includes old printing presses. A literature festival has already
been held in the relatively new museum.
❶ Av. da Autonomia 3; www.facebook.com/mueseuimprensamadeira

There's not much to do in this fishing village. That leaves time for a relaxed game of cards

AROUND CÂMARA DE LOBOS

There are specially fine views of the town and harbour bay from the Pico da Torre viewing point (205m/672ft), above the town to the northeast.

*Pico da Torre

Estreito de Câmara de Lobos lies above Câmara de Lobos at approx. 500m/1640ft and is best known for its excellent wine.
Every autumn, the grape harvest is celebrated in a **wine festival lasting several days**. Its wine tastings and folklore performances have seen the event develop into a real tourist attraction. The **Sunday market** in the town centre, attended by many Madeirans from miles away, is well worth inspecting.

Estreito de Câmara de Lobos

A minor road leads north from Estreito de Câmara de Lobos, reaching Quinta Jardim da Serra (750m/2460ft) after 4km/2.5mi for excellent views and good hiking terrain.

Quinta Jardim da Serra

** CABO GIRÃO

Around 4km beyond Estreito de Câmara de Lobos, a road branches off left to a lookout point across the Cabo Girão. Rising to a height of 580m/1900ft, the cliff face which plummets down to the coast is one of the highest of its kind in Europe – some say, one of the highest in the world. On a clear day there are dizzying views of the small, in

One of Europe's highest cliffs

Hold on tightly! It's easy to get dizzy when looking almost 600m/2000ft down from Cabo Girão

some cases tiny, terraced fields far below the cliff. To the east lie the foothills of Funchal and Câmara de Lobos.

The popular **observation platform** was remodeled in 2012. In the immediate vicinity of Cabo Girão, a new **cable car**, originally built to transport labourers, connects Rancho with the fields along the coast (the trip costs approx. €5). There is a small restaurant with an observation platform at the cable car station.

Further inland, the church of **Nossa Senhora de Fátima** was erected in 1931 and, like the great pilgrimage church on the Portuguese mainland, has a vast square in front of it for assemblies of the faithful.

Boat or elevator There are two ways to reach the beach and small guesthouse of **Fajã dos Padres**, where simple but good food is served – don't miss the cheese cake with pitanga puree! – and where seven cottages are available for overnight guests: by boat or by means of first 187 steps downwards, then an the elevator built into the steep rock face followed by another 181 steps. The reward is a small paradise, a narrow fertile strip of land right on the ocean, densely covered with mango trees, banana plants and pitanga bushes.

Caniçal

✵ C 8

Altitude: 0 – 50m/164ft
Population: approx. 4000

The history of the village of Caniçal on the east coast of Madeira is inextricably linked to that of whaling. Today, the fishermen fill their nets with tuna.

Following massive international protests, whaling ceased here in 1981, where previously 300 whales had been caught and processed per year. A good 200,000 sq km/77,000 sq mi of ocean have now been designated as a marine national park. In order to develop the economy of this barren region after 1981, the government established a free trade zone with a commercial harbour on the site of the earlier whaling station. A large new wharf (for repairs) and an extensive pool complex at the western end of the promenade were also constructed.

Village of whalers

> **MARCO POLO INSIGHT**
>
> ? **Forbidden Souvenir**
>
> In case someone offers whalebone carvings for sale, remember that importing sperm whale bones is illegal in the EU according to the Washington Convention on International Trade in Endangered Species.

WHAT TO SEE IN CANIÇAL

Since 1990, a **whaling museum** keeps the past alive. Originally housed in the former office of the local whalers, the collection received its own modern building on the edge of town in 2011. The museum introduces visitors to the world of whales and shows the important role that whales had in the lives of the islanders in past centuries.

Museu da Baleia

❶ Rua da Pedra d'Eira, Tue – Sun 10am – 6pm, admission: €10, tel. 2 91 96 18 58, www.museudabaleia.org

East of Caniçal, the Capela da Senhora da Piedade stands atop a volcanic rock. Every third weekend in September an impressive **water procession** starts here. A small statue of the Virgin Mary (16th century), probably by a Flemish master, is carried from the chapel to Caniçal along the coast in a colourful procession of boats and back to the chapel.

Capela da Senhora da Piedade

Caniçal

WHERE TO EAT
Cabrestante € – €€ *Insider Tip*
Palmeira Baixo
tel. 2 91 96 00 00
Good fish dishes and an inexpensive daily special; tables ares set up under an umbrella along the street or in the first floor on a balcony – both have a view of the quiet bay.

A Muralha €
Rua da Pedra d'Eira
Banda da Silva
tel. 2 91 96 14 68
The location is not much and the furnishings are pretty plain – but the food is fresh and inexpensive, which attracts many locals as well.

Prainha beach   At the foot of the chapel rock is the diminutive beach of Prainha, which enjoys great popularity with local bathers as the **only natural sandy beach** on Madeira.

Caniço

✦ **D 6/7**

Altitude: 25 – 200m/80 – 650ft
Population: 11,600

Apart from tourism, the main source of income for the inhabitants of Caniço is fruit and vegetable cultivation, hence the proliferation of greenhouses in the area.

Two parishes   The small town of Caniço is situated either side of the river of the same name, just a few miles east of Funchal on the R 101. This narrow watercourse once played an important role: it was the line between the two administrative regions into which Madeira was divided. Caniço thus had two parishes and two churches: the church of the Holy Ghost on the left bank and one dedicated to San Antonio on the right.

Caniço

INFORMATION
Caniço de Baixo
tel. 2 91 93 29 19

WHERE TO EAT
A Lareira €€ – €€€
Estrada da Ponta Oliveira, 2
tel. 2 91 93 44 94
Typically regional dishes, fish – including black scabbardfish with bananas and almonds – and numerous flamed specialities.

Praia Dos Reis Magos € – €€
Beach promenade of Reis Magos
tel. 2 91 93 43 45
It started as a beach bar and has meanwhile been given basalt stone walls, but the furnishings are still modest – just like the food. The portions are large and fresh fish is served often.

WHERE TO STAY
Quinta Splendida €€€ – €€€€
Estrada da Ponta da Oliveira, 11
tel. 2 91 93 04 10
www.quintasplendida.com
166 rooms in various building tracts are grouped around an historical manor house in a 30,000 sq m/ 323,000sq ft botanical garden. Large spa.

Insider Tip

Oásis Four Views Hotel €€ – €€€
Praia dos Reis Magos
tel. 2 91 93 01 00
www.fourviewshotels.com
Completely renovated, ecological (solar power, water treatment) house with 220 rooms. The Oásis Four Views Hotel is right on the beach promenade, has a garden, a beautiful pool landscape and a wellness spa.

Prainha, the only natural sand beach on Madeira, is located at Caniçal

WHAT TO SEE IN CANIÇO

The village square, beautifully paved with basalt mosaic stones, is a meeting point for the local people. Here stands the **parish church**, with a dedication inscribed above the portal to the Holy Ghost and San Antonio – although the parishes were united as long ago as the 15th century, the ruinous churches were only torn down and the present structure erected in the 18th century. Also on the village square is the 16th-century **Manueline chapel** of Madre de Deus.

Village square

At the southern edge of the village lie the grounds of the Quinta Splendida estate. A country residence which has been tastefully converted into a hotel, it is furnished with a wealth of antiques and houses a **gourmet restaurant**. The magnificent, beautifully landscaped park is well worth a visit.

*Quinta Splendida

Approximately 3km/2mi below Caniço, Caniço de Baixo has developed into Madeira's most important tourist centre alongside Funchal, with an infrastructure to match yet without being overrun. Set

Caniço de Baixo

into the rock, the **seawater bathing pools** of Rocamar and Galomar are suitable for diving and are open to the public as well as hotel guests. Another place to go swimming is the pebble beach of Reis Magos with a beach promenade and several hotels, on the eastern perimeter of the village, as the presence of many Madeirans testifies.

Ponta do Garajau

Leaving Caniço in a southwesterly direction, a road winds its way down to Ponta do Garajau and a huge **statue of Christ**, built in 1927. From the terrace in front, there are far-reaching views across to the bay of Funchal.

Marine national park

The sea beyond Ponta do Garajau, between Ponta da Oliveira (in the east) and São Gonçalo (in the west) is an environmentally protected area called the Reserva Natural Parcial do Garajau. This **paradise for divers** is also populated by groupers, and the sight of an elegant manta gliding through the water is not unusual, particularly in late summer.

✶✶ Curral das Freiras

 C 5

Altitude: 690 – 990m/2260 – 3248ft
Population: 2000

Curral das Freiras – literally »Valley of the Nuns« – is one of Madeira's most impressive landscapes. The most commanding view of this scenery can be enjoyed when approaching from Eira do Serrado.

Valley of the Nuns

Both the valley and the village were given their name by the **nuns of the Santa Clara convent in Funchal**, who retreated here in 1566 following an attack by French corsairs. In earlier times, the almost circular Curral das Freiras was thought to be an extinct volcanic crater. More recent research suggests it is merely a product of erosion: the river which now runs through the valley has taken the soft tuff with it through the ages, whilst the harder basalt of the steep rock face remains.

The valley of Curral das Freiras was already cultivated by nuns of the Santa Clara convent before the corsairs' attack in 1566, but the village was only established some 200 years later. In the 19th century, nuns had the church of Nossa Senhora do Livramento built at the southern edge of the village centre. The **magnificent landscape as seen from the village** is certain to impress. In addition to grain, wine and fruit, especially chestnuts, tourism plays an increasing role. Souvenir shops and cafés are clustered around the village square.

Curral das Freiras

WHERE TO EAT
Parada dos Eucaliptos €
Estrada da Eira do Serrado, 258
tel. 2 91 77 68 88
Family-run business with typical, fresh-ly prepared dishes like skewers pre-pared in an oven, bolo de caco, milho frito, along with an acceptable house wine.

WHERE TO STAY
Estalagem Eira **Insider**
do Serrado €€ **Tip**
Eira do Serrado

tel. 2 91 72 42 20
www.eiradoserrado.com
25 rooms
Comfortable mountain hotel with a res-taurant in a remote location. Peace and quiet guaranteed at night, but daytimes can get very touristy.

FESTIVAL
Chestnuts are the speciality in Curral das Freiras. Festa das Castanhas, which of-fers anything to do with chestnuts, takes place every year on 1 November.

Passing through the eucalyptus forest, dense in places, on the way from Funchal to Curral das Freiras, Eira do Serrado is reached (Ser-rado saddle; 1026m/3366ft) at the northeastern edge of the Pico do Serrado. Along the way, a road branches off to the right to a moun-tain hotel (1km/half a mile), where the car park leads to a pleasant, shady forest trail and on to a panoramic platform, high above the Curral Valley. Visitors can gaze **from a dizzying height** into the deep basin below.

***View from Eira do Serrado**

Those with enough stamina and a good head for heights can follow a trail down to Curral das Freiras; the hike is worthwhile and takes around one and a half hours. A bus leaves from the village church if the journey back up proves a little daunting.

Faial

✦ B 6

Altitude: approx. 150m/490ft
Population: 1600 (Faial), 2600 (Porto da Cruz)

The pretty little town of Faial lies high above the northeast coast amidst fertile fruit and vegetable gardens. Wine grow-ing is also of economic importance. This region's rural pros-perity is manifested in the well-kept houses of Faial, which gets its name from the many myrica faya trees in the region. The larger town of Porto da Cruz is located down on the coast.

A prominent cliff – Eagle Rock near Faial. The eastern point of Madeira can be seen in the distance

WHAT TO SEE IN AND AROUND FAIAL

Eagle Rock The church vestibule provides lovely views of Madeira's northern coast, with Faial's own landmark, Eagle Rock (Penha de Águia, 594m/1948ft), an isolated, almost **cubic cliff towering into the sky**. The name is a reference to the ospreys who nest in its heights. For a time, they were thought to have died out on Madeira, but happily they have been sighted again more recently.

Swim and splash Praia do Faial, an artificial **lagoon** at the mouth of the Ribeira São Roque do Faial, attracts swimmers with on-site changing rooms, a children's playground and deck chairs for rent.

Fortim do Faial

Insider Tip

Fortim do Faial is a local gem on the road to Santana, a defence post against pirates that was built in the 18th century, equipped with seven English cannon. Old photographs and etchings in the small fort recall the island in former times. There is a wonderful view from here.

Faial

WHERE TO EAT
Esplanada Praça do Engenho € – €€
Casas Próximas, Rua Sousa Dias
Porto da Cruz, tel. 2 91 56 36 80
Typical local cooking, good fish dishes.

WHERE TO SLEEP
Costa Linda €€
Rua Dr. Abel de Freitas, Porto da Cruz
tel. 2 91 56 00 80, 2 91 56 00 89
www.costa-linda.net
13 small, simple rooms, most of them

have a balcony and a view of the ocean.
To reach the ocean and seawater pools is
takes only a few steps across the street, a
bus stop is about 200m/700ft away.

Quinta da Capela €€   **Insider Tip**
Sítio do Folhada, Porto da Cruz
tel. 2 91 72 42 36, 2 91 23 53 97
www.villasmadeira.com
Historic manor house above the town,
five rooms with antique furnishings and
a beautiful garden.

Porto da Cruz– east of Faial, on the coast beyond Eagle Rock – is an   **Porto da Cruz**
attractive little place with a **seawater swimming pool** down in the
bay. Higher up, next to the church, is a panoramic terrace with beautiful views of the bay, the remains of an old fort on the rocks jutting
out from the coast and a sugar factory chimney – Porto da Cruz was,
for many years, a **centre of sugarcane cultivation**.

** Funchal

✴ **D 5/6**

Altitude: 0 – 550m/1800ft
Population: 112,000

**The capital of Madeira has an unusually beautiful location on
the southern coast of the island. The houses and streets line the
slopes of a mountain range which rises to some 1200m/3900ft.
A stroll through the streets of the old town or along the harbour can be as rewarding as a visit to the city's churches, palaces and museums, whilst the rich subtropical vegetation
found in splendid gardens is truly something to behold.**

Funchal and its surrounding area are the vibrant centre of the island,   **Vibrant**
home to around half the people of Madeira. The city is the adminis-   **centre**
trative centre of the Região Autónoma da Madeira, a trade and bank-
ing centre, the seat of a Roman Catholic bishop and a university city.
The archipelago's only sizeable harbour is here – once an important
hub for international transatlantic shipping, it is now primarily frequented by cruise ships.

Tourism Tourism is concentrated in the western part of town, where a veritable **hotel zone** has developed, consisting largely of 3-star to 5-star hotels. Funchal is also where Madeira's nightlife plays out: evening entertainments include a casino, cinema and theatre.

History Before people could settle in Funchal, fires were set to clear the bay of fennel. João Gonçalves Zarco was allotted the west of Madeira in 1450 and initially made Câmara de Lobos his base, before later settling in Funchal. The eastern part of Madeira was governed by the administration in Machico. King Manuel I put an end to the partition of the island in 1497, declaring Funchal its capital. The history of Funchal is, by and large, synonymous with that of Madeira, as it profited from the boom in sugar trade and was the chief trading centre for Madeira wine – the city's coat of arms thus shows five sugar loaves and grapes. It did not take long for Funchal to become the **focal point of Madeiran tourism**, as it still is today.

Highlights Funchal

► **Cathedral**
The fantastic cedar wood ceiling is one of the most beautiful in all of Portugal.
►page 144

► **Mercado dos Lavradores**
Fruit and vegetables, fish and cheese on all sides.
►page 151

► **Cable car to Monte**
The glass cabins of the teleférico offer a glorious panoramic view.
►page 151, 169

► **Madeira Wine Company**
Learn all about the famous Madeira wine here.
►page 145

► **Museum for sacred art**
What sugar used to buy you...
►page 154

► **Embroidery museum**
The state institute for arts and crafts has accumulated a respectable collection of Madeira embroidery.
►page 153

► **Quinta das Cruzes**
This museum shows some of the island's cultural history; the stone masonry and the wonderful collection of orchids in the opulent gardens attract many visitors.
►page 156

► **Reid's Palace**
A hotel with a tradition, where numerous illustrious guests from all over the world have stopped.
►page 68, 159

► **Jardim Botânico**
Local and tropical plants surround a small museum of natural history in a manor house.
►page 159

BETWEEN AVENIDA DO MAR AND AVENIDA ARRIAGA

The harbour is the ideal place to commence a walk through Funchal's centre. Here, where ships bound for Brazil and India came into port in years gone by, the attractive promenade Avenida do Mar now extends along the seafront. Vast cruise ships can be seen across the marina. A row of bars and boat excursion operators await the tourists. Sightseeing tours depart from above the marina.

Harbour

Insider Tip

Madeira's first fortress, the Fortaleza de São Lourenço, stands on Avenida do Mar. It was built in the 16th century on the site of older, rudimentary defences and has been rebuilt on a number of occasions.

Fortaleza de São Lourenço

In the evening the Bay of Funchal becomes a glittering sea of light

Today it serves as residence for the Minister of the Republic, Portugal's representative on Madeira. The mighty 18th-century sea façade of the eastern tower displays the Portuguese emblem with the cross of the Order of the Knights of Christ, the Portuguese successors to the Knights Templar, and two armillary spheres. These nautical devices symbolize Portugal's era of discovery.

Alfândega Velha (Old Customs House) Further to the east is the Old Customs House (Alfândega Velha). Little remains of the original construction of 1477. Having been almost completely destroyed by an earthquake in 1748, it was rebuilt and extended in the 18th century. The rather unostentatious entrance on the rear side of the building (▶p. 51) is considered a **fine specimen of Manueline architecture**.

Cathedral (Sé) Funchal's cathedral, known as Sé in Portuguese (from the Latin *sedes* = see, seat), is reached via the pretty pedestrian zone in Rua João Tavira. In 1514 it became the first overseas Portuguese cathedral to be consecrated.

Its rather plain, almost austere exterior is characterized by the contrast of white plaster and dark basalt. A decorative rosette is emblazoned above the Gothic main portal. Higher up, at the very top is a **cross of the Order of Christ**, of which King Manuel I was Grand Master – this cross is also still an element in the flag of Madeira. The mighty, rectangular main tower is crowned by a pyramidal roof with geometrically arranged tiles.

Inside, the cathedral impresses in many respects: the high altar and the eight side altars of the basilica with its nave and two aisles were brought from Flanders in the 16th century, as were the choir stalls. They were paid for from the proceeds of the sugar trade, so lucrative at the time. Particularly worthy of note is the magnificent Mudéjar-style ceiling, artfully carved from local wood. The **keystones in the choir vault**, with the cross of the Order of Christ, the Portuguese crest and the armillary sphere (▶Fortaleza de São Lourenço) are quite beautiful.

❶ Daily 8am – 12noon and 4pm – 6.30pm

? MARCO ⊕ POLO INSIGHT

»Flower costumes«

The flower market next to the Late Gothic cathedral has been held for many years. The flower sellers, who are called »flower girls«, are required by law to wear their traditional costumes while they work.

Insider Tip

»The City of Sugar« East of the cathedral lies Praça de Colombo, its centre decorated with a mosaic of the Funchal coat of arms. The Núcleo Museológico »A Cidade do Açucar« shows the most precious **craft artefacts from the heyday of the sugar trade**, namely the 15th and 16th centuries; here it is possible to see what could be purchased with the profits from the sugar boom.

Also on display are items excavated from a neighbouring house which once belonged to a Flemish sugar trader in which Columbus is said to have stayed.

❶ Currently closed

West of the cathedral, Avenida Arriaga runs northwards, parallel to Avenida do Mar. This lively street in the town centre, now partly pedestrianized, is awash with vivid blue and violet jacaranda blossoms. At the crossroads with Avenida Zarco, a (1934) monument by Francisco Franco honours the island's discoverer, João Gonçalves Zarco (▶p. 166).

Avenida Arriaga

Housed in a former Franciscan monastery opposite the Fortaleza de São Lourenço and next to the tourist information office, the Madeira Wine Company has **the oldest and most important wine cellar on Madeira**. Guided tours explain how Madeira wine is made (groups should book in advance). To round things off in the nicest possible fashion, there are two tasting rooms where the wine may be sampled and, of course, purchased. A small museum adjacent displays old letters and documents, along with historical tools.

**Madeira Wine Company

❶ Mon – Fri 10am – 6.30pm, Sat 10am – 1pm, admission: €5, tours Mon – Fri several times a day, Sat 11am, book a tour on the website www.theoldblandywinelodge.com or tel. 2 91 74 01 10

Next to the Madeira Wine Company are the lush tropical plants of the **municipal gardens**, created in 1878 on the site of the monastery gardens. The stone coat of arms of the Franciscan order can be seen in the southeast corner of the grounds.

*Jardim Municipal

In 1982 a statue of Francis of Assisi was erected in honour of his 800th birthday.

A popular photo opportunity is a statue of two boys playing at the duck pond. Two interesting buildings stand opposite: one is the Chamber of Commerce, embellished with a blue and white, tiled façade depicting **typical motifs of the island**. The other is the **municipal theatre** (Teatro Municipal), established in 1888. As well as plays and films, art exhibitions and concerts are also staged here.

> ! **MARCO❂POLO TIP**
>
> *Mini-Eco Bar* **Insider Tip**
>
> Up-market location with ecological claims: from the wall paint through waste recycling down to the furnishings made of cast off household objects. Café during the daytime, popular club with music in the evenings (Rua da Alfândega, 3, tel. 9 18 69 60 02, www.fresh-citrus.com).

A little further on, at **Diogo's Wine Spirits Shop**, books, maps and copperplate engravings concerning Christopher Columbus can be viewed. They were collected from all over the world by the shop's founder and now comprise a small museum.

Museu Cristóvão

❶ Mon – Fri 9.30am – 1pm and 3pm – 7pm, Sat 9.30am – 1pm, admission €2.

Funchal

INFORMATION
Direcção Regional do Turismo – Região Autónoma da Madeira
Avenida M. Arriaga, 18
P-9004-519 Funchal
tel. 2 91 21 19 02
www.visitmadeira.pt

Madeira Maritime Station
(quay for cruise ships)
tel. 2 91 77 52 54

TRANSPORT
Driving is no fun here, especially during rush hours, and parking places are rare. From Funchal's hotel zone it is better to go into town on the hotel's shuttle bus or the orange city bus (inexpensive 7-day ticket) and to explore the centre on foot. Good shoes are advised because of the sometimes uneven and slippery cobblestones. Most buses stop down at the harbour on Avenida do Mar, which is also a good starting point for a walking tour.

SIGHTSEEING
An open doubledecker bus leaves on the hour (Mar – Oct) or every 90 minutes (Nov – Feb) to tour Funchal with explanations in English; departure from Avenida do Mar near the harbour.

SHOPPING
In Funchal's old city there are countless shops, from international chains to what-not shops. The shopping street Rua do Aljube is located north of the cathedral; it leads to the department store Bazar do Povo, which opened in 1883. Rua Dr. Fernão Ornelas west of the market hall is another major shopping street. Diverse shopping centres invite strolling, like the Marina Shopping Centre at the harbour, the Eden Mar and the Monumental Lido in the hotel zone above the Lido, the Centromar in the south-west as well as the Dolce Vita not far from Praça do Infante.

FEAST AND FESTIVAL
Festa da Flor
In April the fantastic flower festival greets the Spring.

Festival do Atlântico
In June the Festival offers classical music concerts, ballet and folklore events.

GOING OUT
Young people congregate at the disco »Vespas« after midnight, while their seniors go to the disco »O Farol« (Hotel Pestana Carlton Madeira) on Fridays and Saturdays after 11pm or in the casino nightclub »Copacabana«. Jazz can be heard live at »jam – Jazz & Music Lounge« or in the »Moonlight Bar« of the hotel »Tivoli Ocean Park«.

CAFES
Grand Café Golden Gate
Avenida Arriaga, 29
tel. 2 91 23 43 83
Seeing and being seen – with a »bica« or a beer. Lunch is served middays in the first floor.

Café do Teatro
Avenida Arriaga
Quite elegant café bar downstairs in the city theatre; beautiful inner courtyard.

WHERE TO EAT

❶ *Il Gallo d' Oro* €€€€

Estrada Monumental, 147
The Cliff Bay
tel. 2 91 70 77 00
Ever since 2009 Benoît Sinthon has had
a Michelin star at the »Golden Rooster«
– it is the only one on Madeira. But the
cuisine (Mediterranean, local products
as well as international) and service
don't always live up to it.

❷ *Armazém do Sal* €€€ – €€€€

Rua da Alfândega, 135
tel. 2 91 24 12 85
www.armazemdosal.com
Fish from octopus out of the oven to bacalhau with an herb crust, surf & turf,
interesting side dishes.

❸ *Restaurante da Forte* €€€

Rua Portão de São Tiago
tel. 2 91 21 55 80
Portuguese cooking in modern variations and in a romantic setting – depending on which room of the harbour
fortress you happen to be sitting in.

❹ *Riso* €€ – €€€

Rua Santa Maria, 274
tel. 2 91 28 03 60
It's all about rice – from goat cheese ri-
sotto to Madeira tiramisu. Fabulous location above the sea!

❺ *Combatentes* €€ – €€€ *Insider Tip*

Rua Ivens, 1
tel. 2 91 22 1388
The small formal city restaurant at the
Jardim Municipal serves good regional
and international food.

❻ *Lareira Portuguesa* €€ – €€€

Travessa Doutor Valente, 7
tel. 2 91 76 29 11
Restaurant with a varied selection made
from local products, which convinces
both in taste and in appearance. Extensive wine cellar.

❼ *O Portão* €€ – €€€

Rua Portão de São Tiago
tel. 2 91 22 11 25
Low key ambience, nice service and
good, solid cooking.

❽ *Café do Museu* €€ *Insider Tip*

Praça do Município, tel. 2 91 28 11 21
Popular lunch spot, friendly service.
Excellent tuna carpaccio or vegetarian
lasagna are on the menu.

❾ *A Bica* € – €€

Rua do Hospital Velho, 17
Freshly prepared, typical Madeiran food,
including less well-known dishes. Good
homemade desserts.

❿ *Frutaria Cidade Velha* €

Rua de Santa Maria, 67
tel. 2 91 22 10 42
Two shops, one name: fruit and vegetables are sold here, eaten there: soups,
sandwiches, omelettes, Madeira burgers
and various other local specialities.

WHERE TO STAY

❶ *Reid's Palace Hotel* €€€€

Estrada Monumental, 139
tel. 291 717 171
www.reidspalace.com; 169 Z.
For more than 115 years the legendary
Reid's has been the first address on
Madeira (► MARCO POLO Insight, p. 68).

Funchal

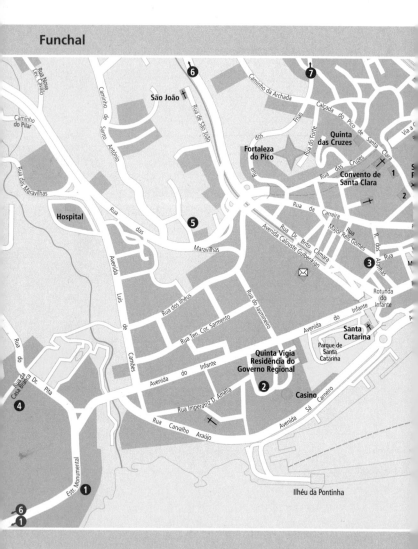

1 Museu Frederico de Freitas
2 Museu Municipal
3 Museu Photographia Vicentes
4 Câmara Municipal
5 Museu de Arte Sacra

6 Madeira Wine Company
7 Teatro Municipal
8 Alfândega Velha
9 Centro Museológico do Açúcar
10 IBTAM

Capela da Encarnação

Museu Henrique e Francisco Franco

Museu do Vinho

Igreja do Colégio

Governo Regional

Fortaleza São Lourenco

Mercado
Catedral Sé

Museu de Electricidade

Teleférico Funchal-Monte

Mercado dos Lavradores

Estadio

Igreja do Socorro

Fortaleza de São Tiago
Museu de Arte Contemporânea

Bahia de Funchal

Molhe da Pontinha

Porto Santo →

250 m

©BAEDEKER

Where to eat

1 Il Galo d'Oro
2 Armazém do Sal
3 Restaurante da Forte
4 Riso
5 Combatentes
6 Lareira Portuguesa
7 O Portão
8 Café do Museu
9 A Bica
10 Frutaria Cidade Velha

Where to stay

1 Reid's Palace Hotel
2 Hotel Pestana Casino Park
3 The Vine
4 Quinta da Casa Branca
5 Quintinha de São João
6 Estalagem Quinta da Bela Vista
7 Quinta Jardins do Lago
8 Molhe Hotel – Conde Carvalhal
9 Hotel do Carmo
10 Pensão Astória

❷ Hotel Pestana Casino Park €€€€
Rua Imperatriz D. Amélia, 55
tel. 2 91 20 91 00
www.pestana.com
The concrete structure by the architect Oscar Niemeyer is one of the best addresses on Madeira. 373 large rooms, many with an ocean view; sports, entertainment.

❸ The Vine €€€€
Rua dos Aranhas, 27-A
tel. 2 91 00 90 00
www.hotelthevine.com; 79 rooms
Design hotel, integrated into a shopping centre with a spa, rooftop pool and a good restaurant.

❹ Quinta da Casa Branca €€€€
Rua da Casa Branca, 5-7
tel. 2 91 70 07 70
www.quintacasabranca.pt
This quinta is an oasis of rest in a wonderful garden, located in an old manor house and in a discreetly designed modern part. There are 41 rooms in all and two suites, a spa, sauna, a heated pool and two restaurants, Casa da Quinta and Garden Pavilion.

❺ Quintinha de São João €€€ – €€€€
Rua da Levada de São João, 4
tel. 2 91 74 09 20
www.quintinhasaojoao.com
Pretty hotel in a cultivated country style with comfortably furnished rooms. a swimming pool, spa area, restaurant and a bar.

❻ Estalagem Quinta da Bela Vista €€€ – €€€€
Caminho do Avista Navios, 4
tel. 2 91 70 64 00
www.belavistamadeira.com; 89 Z.
Family-owned quinta located above the city. There is a beautiful view of the sea and the mountains.

❼ Quinta Jardins do Lago €€€
Rua Dr. João Lemos Gomes, 29
São Pedro, tel. 2 91 75 01 00
www.jardins-lago.pt
40 elegant rooms and suites in an old quinta with a beautiful garden.

❽ Molhe Hotel – Conde Carvalhal €€
Rua Conde de Carvalhal, 53
tel. 2 91 72 14 03
www.molhehotelcondecarvalhal.com
Quinta with a modern extension. Some rooms have a kitchenette; some have a nice view over Funchal below.

❾ Hotel do Carmo €€ *Insider Tip*
Travessa do Rego, 10
tel. 2 91 20 12 40
www.hoteldocarmomadeira.com
Located in the heart of the city with a pool on the roof terrace and a view of the Atlantic. Some of the 80 rooms reflect nostalgically back on the 1960s thanks to the large black-and-white posters of movie scenes.

❿ Pensão Astória €
Rua João Gago,10
tel. 2 91 22 38 20
www.pensaoastoria.com
Less than 100m/330ft away from the cathedral; simple accommodations in the 4th floor of an historic house.

Avenida Arriaga ends at the **Rotunda do Infante**, named after Henry the Navigator (▶Famous People), at whose behest of João Gonçalves Zarco reconnoitred Madeira in 1419. The monument, the work of Francisco Franco, was erected in 1947.

Monument to Henry the Navigator

EASTERN CITY CENTRE

One of Funchal's most splendid sights is the market hall, named »Mercado dos Lavradores« (peasants' market). The blue and white tiled frescoes at the main entrance portray scenes of market life. Inside, the stalls are packed with an unbelievable **abundance of marvellous fruit** on two levels around a broad court, its walls similarly adorned with tiled frescoes. The lower level is dedicated to local producers on Friday and Saturday mornings. In the first floor the prices are higher and the salespeople are pushier. In the eastern section, the fish market building in characteristic 1930s design is above all devoted to delicious tuna and scabbard fish.

**Market hall – Mercado dos Lavradores

❶ Mon – Fri 8am – 8pm, Sat 7am – 2pm

MARCO ⊕ POLO TIP

! *Market Christmas* **Insider Tip**

On December 23 Mercado dos Lavradores is filled with a special atmosphere. In the afternoon already the surrounding streets are closed off; booths and stands are put up and in the market hall everything is taken out of the fish department. Then thousands of people gather for the »Noite de Mercado« in order to sing Christmas songs together.

South of the market hall, towards the sea, the **Praça da Autonomia** monument commemorates the **Carnation Revolution of 1974** and the successful attainment of autonomy for Madeira. At the eastern edge stands the highly interesting **Museu da Electricidade**, offering an excellent insight into the development of electricity on Madeira. A splendid model of the island graphically illustrates by means of small lamps how illumination progressed from 1897 to 1997.

❶ 10am – 12.30pm and 2pm – 6pm, daily, admission: €2.70.

Immediately to the southeast of the market hall, the Old Town of Funchal begins, once a **district of fishermen and artisans**. Some of its small shops and narrow alleyways still leave a rather humble impression. Attempts are being made to improve the local infrastructure with the help of public investment. There is a small area geared to tourists with a few restaurants. Right in the south is the valley station of the **teleférico**, the cable car to Monte.

*Zona Velha (Old Town)

A worthy addition to the Praça Almirante Reis is the new **Madeira Story Centre**. This themed centre in the former Santa Maria cinema and erstwhile storehouse of the agricultural society takes visitors on

a virtual journey to Madeira's past and its development up to the present day.

❶ 10am–6pm daily, admission: €9.60, combination ticket with Old Blandy Wine Lodge: €12.50, www.storycentre.com

At the eastern border of the **Zona Velha** (Old City), the picturesque Fortaleza de São Tiago stands watch over the small harbour bay of the former fishing district. Work began on the site in 1614, with considerable extensions added in 1767. A small military exhibition is joined by the **Museu de Arte Contemporânea** (Museum for Contemporary Art), which shows changing exhibitions of Portuguese painters since around 1960 and a permanent collection of works by the artist Lourdes de Castro.

*Fortaleza de São Tiago

❶ Mon–Sat 10am–12.30pm and 2pm–5.30pm, admission: €3.

> **MARCO⊕POLO TIP**
>
> ! *Delicate treasures*   Insider Tip
>
> In Rua Visconde Anadia, 33/34 is the largest embroidery factory on Madeira, Patrício & Gouveia. A tour reveals the immense amount of work that goes into the high quality produced here in fantastic white and needlepoint embroidery, all of which has its price too (Mon to Fri 9am–1pm and 3pm to 6.30pm, Sat 9.30am–12noon).

A short distance behind the Fortaleza de São Tiago stands the Igreja do Socorro (Church of the Redeemer), also known as Santa Maria Maior, the parish church of the Old Town. Originally built in the 16th century, the church was dedicated to Saint James the Younger, the patron saint of Funchal, who, according to legend, saved the town from the plague in 1538. Largely destroyed by the earthquake of 1748, the present structure is richly adorned with Baroque art and carvings and now dedicated to the Mother of God. Nevertheless, there is an annual procession in honour of St James on 1 May.

Igreja do Socorro

Barreirinha Lido, situated below the Igreja do Socorro, entices bathers with its pools, flume, sunbathing area, bar and restaurant.

Barreirinha Lido

Further north on Rua Visconde Anadia, in the so-called »district between the rivers«, an Embroidery Museum has been installed in rooms belonging to IVBAM (Instituto do Vinho, do Bordado e Artesanto da Madeira), Madeira's institute for handicrafts. Examples of embroidery from the 19th century are on display, including christening robes and children's clothes from wealthy Madeiran families, as well as contemporary items.

Embroidery Museum

❶ Rua Visconde anadia, 44, Mon–Fri 10am–12.30pm and 2pm–5.30pm, admission: €2.

Like paradise – fruit and vegetables in all shapes and sizes in the Funchal market hall

Museu Henrique e Francisco Franco   The Museu Henrique e Francisco Franco showcases works by two brothers. Francisco Franco began his career as a sculptor in Rodin's circle in Paris and later came under criticism for his proximity to the Salazar dictatorship. His brother Henrique was a painter.

❶ Mon – Fri 10am – 12.30pm and 2pm – 6pm, admission: €3.70.

NORTH OF AVENIDA ARRIAGA

*Praça do Município   To the north of the cathedral, the Praça do Município or **town hall square** is decoratively paved and graced with a fountain. It is bordered by a harmonious ensemble of Baroque houses. On the eastern side of the square stands the **town hall** (Câmara Municipal), built in 1758 as the residence of the Conde de Carvalhal, one of Madeira's richest families at the time, before it passed into the hands of the municipal administration at the end of the 19th century. The foyer is decorated with Baroque azulejos, the courtyard adorned by a sculpture, Leda and Zeus as a Swan. The tower served as an observation point from which to identify incoming trade ships at the earliest opportunity.

On the northwest side, the **Igreja do Colégio**, a 17th-century church of the former Jesuit College, has disappointingly irregular opening hours. Its remarkable interior is resplendent with gilded carvings and azulejos. This former college of the Jesuit order, where sons of rich Madeirans once studied, is now the seat of the **University** of Madeira.

? MARCO ⊕ POLO INSIGHT

Henry the German

The painting of St Joachim and St Anne in the museum for sacred art (Museu de Arte Sacra) is supposed to portray King Wladislaw of Poland, who is better known on Madeira as Henry the German, and his wife.

Museu de Arte Sacra   On the southern side of the square, the Museum for Sacred Art has been housed since 1955 in what used to be the bishop's palace (17th century). The extraordinary **collection of Flemish art from the 15th and 16th centuries shows just how valuable sugar once was. It includes pieces by Rogier van der Weyden, taken as payment for sugar shipped from Madeira. Also well worth seeing are the precious items in the cathedral treasury, including an intricately crafted, gold-plated silver Manueline processional cross. The Café do Museu is a popular rendezvous for art aficionados and others.

❶ Tue – Sat 10am – 12.30pm and 2.30pm – 6pm, Sun 10am – 1pm; admission: €3, www.museuartesacrafunchal.org

*Museu Photographia Vicentes   A visit to Vicentes, the photography museum to the west of the town hall square, is an absolute treat. Vicente Gomes da Silva founded the **first photographic studio in Portugal** in 1848. His son, grandson and great grandson continued his work. As well as the original furnishings, with old optical and photographic devices, historic photos of Madeira and its inhabitants are on display, including Empress Elisabeth of Austria. The museum also houses a large photography archive.

Insider Tip

❶ Rua da Carreira 43, Mon – Fri 10am – 12.30pm and 2pm – 5pm, admission: €3, www.photographiamuseuvicentes.com.pt

The nave of the Igreja de São Pedro is decorated almost entirely with tiles from the 17th century, whilst the gilded altar is no less impressive.

Opposite, inside the 18th-century Palácio de São Pedro, once the town residence of the Condes de Carvalhal, is the **Natural History Museum**. The aquarium on the ground floor presents the underwater flora and fauna of Madeira, and the upper level houses an extensive taxidermy collection reflecting Madeira's rich array of animal life.

Church and Palace of São Pedro

❶ Tue – Fri 10am – 6pm, Sat/Sun noon – 6pm, admission: €3.50

The wealthy lawyer Dr. Frederico de Freitasacquired the 17th-century residence of the Counts of Calçada in the 1940s and bequeathed it to the town on his death in 1978, complete with his extensive **arts and crafts collections**, which he had built up over many years. Faithfully maintained in the style of various epochs, the house displays furniture, paintings and everyday artefacts. The adjacent Casa dos Azulejos is home to the patron's impressive collection of tiles.

**Frederico de Freitas collections

❶ Tue – Sat 10am – 12.30pm and 2pm – 5.30pm, admission €3

The granddaughters of the island's discoverer, Zarco, probably had the Santa Clara Convent built at the end of the 15th century as a cloister for **sisters of the Order of Saint Clare**. It is situated at the top of Calçada de Santa Clara. As time progressed, the nuns came to wield considerable influence; due in no small measure to endowments, the landed estates of the convent were sizeable. The wine trade also contributed to the fortune of the Santa Clara nuns. When French corsairs invaded Funchal in 1566, pillaging the convent in the process, the nuns fled to ▶Curral das Freiras. Following the death of the last sister of the Order of Saint Clare in 1890, **Franciscan nuns** took over the cloister; today they run a daycare centre here, among other things. The convent's appearance is still largely defined by the alterations and extensions undertaken in the 17th century. The Gothic portal of the convent church and the cloister with a winged altar are surviving elements of the 16th-century original construction.

**Convento de Santa Clara

The interior of the church is **completely tiled with blue, white and yellow azulejos from the 16th and 17th centuries**. The discoverer of the island, Zarco, and members of his family are buried in the

A charming villa: Quinta das Cruzes

chancel. Towards the rear of the nave, with its decorative, painted wood-panelled ceiling, is the Manueline-style tomb of Zarco's son-in-law, Mendes de Vasconcelos. Visitors are accompanied by a guide through the convent (please ring the bell).

❶ Mon – Fri 10am – noon and 3pm – 5pm, admission: €2

**Quinta das Cruzes

Above the convent stands the Quinta das Cruzes. It is thought to date back to the 15th century, when it served as the residence of Zarco, the explorer who discovered the island. Destroyed to a large extent by the earthquake of 1748, it was reconstructed at the end of the 18th century.

Since 1953 it has housed a **museum of cultural history**, offering insight into the lives of affluent Madeirans from the 16th to the 19th century. Items worthy of note are sugar-chest furniture, azulejos, porcelain and silver. It is worth attending one of the concerts staged here now and again just to savour the lovely atmosphere.

The former residence is surrounded by a **park noted for the splendid old trees within its grounds**. Examples of stonemasonry collected from all over the island from the 15th to the 19th century are also gathered here, including Funchal's old pillory and two Manueline window arches. The orchid collection in the upper section of the park is well worth seeing.

❶ Tue – Sun 10am – 12.30pm and 2pm – 5.30pm, admission: €3, www.museuquintadascruzes.com

Those who like a good walk can march up the hill to the imposing Fortaleza do Pico (17th century), with a nautical radar station and a mini-museum, and enjoy the magnificent panorama of Funchal and the bay.

Fortaleza do Pico

❶ 9am – 6pm daily, free admission

On the west side of Rua da Carreira (no. 235), the **British Cemetery** is worth a visit. It dates back to the English occupation of Madeira (1807 – 1814); up to that time, the burial of non-Catholics and the practice of religion other than Roman Catholicism were forbidden on the island. Amongst the plots that can be found here is the family tomb of the **Blandy merchant family**, along with the grave of **William Reid**, who founded the hotel of the same name (▶Famous People).

*Cemitério Británico

❶ Mon – Fri 8.30am – 5pm; regrettably, the cemetery is often closed in spite of the public opening hours

WEST OF THE ROTUNDA DO INFANTE

West of the Rotunda do Infante, the delightful Parque de Santa Catarina was created in the mid-20th century. It is a beautiful municipal park with flower beds, aviaries, a swan pond, a café and panoramic terrace with excellent views of the harbour. The small and simple **Capela de Santa Catarina** goes back to the 17th century. A statue of Christopher Columbus gazing into the distance stands alongside the chapel.
The park features two better known **sculptures by Francisco Franco**: the bronze statue *The Sower* and – towards the harbour – a monument to the two Portuguese pilots who made the first air crossing from Lisbon to Madeira in 1921.

*Parque de Santa Catarina

Insider Tip

Beneath the Parque de Santa Catarina lies the harbour wall of the **Pontinha pier**, where cruise ships and the ferry to Porto Santo berth. Somewhat further to the west, anchored in the cargo harbour – if not out to sea – is the Santa Maria, a replica of the sailing vessel of the same name with which Christopher Columbus sailed to America (▶p. 73, 111).

Harbour jetty Pontinha

The pink-walled Quinta Vigia (formerly the Quinta das Angústias) on the west side of the Parque de Santa Catarina is now the **official residence of the regional president** and, as such, is not open to visitors. Its attractive grounds, which include a viewing terrace, are open to the public however, even during state visits. The original Quinta Vigia stood on the land adjacent but had to make way for the Casino and Pestana Casino Park Hotel, both designed by the Brazil-

*Quinta Vigia

ian architect Oscar Niemeyer. Another resident in the Quinta Vigia of old was the Empress of Austria and Queen of Hungary, (▶Famous People), who is commemorated by a bronze statue next to the hotel looking onto Avenida do Infante.

Casino   The Funchal casino, a round cement building, resembles the cathedral of Brasília, which was also designed by Oscar Niemeyer and which is supposed to similar to a crown of thorns. The architect, who was born in Rio de Janeiro in 1907, is considered to be one of the pioneers of modern architecture. His unusual works are often characterized by generous, widely sweeping. The hotel next to the casino is also his work.

❶ Avenida do Infante, Sun – Thu 3pm – 3am, Fri and Sat 4pm – 4am, tel. 291140424, www.casinodamadeira.com

The casino in Funchal was designed by the Brazilian architect Oscar Niemeyer

A museum for fans of Cristiano Ronaldo: the star football player from Funchal exhibits his collection of trophies, videos and pictures here.

CR7

❶ Rua Princesa D. Amélia, 10; Mon – Sat 10am – 6pm; admission: €5

South of the Quinta Magnólia, directly on the coast, stands the time-honoured **Reid's** Hotel (▶MARCO POLO Insight, p. 68). Beyond the hotel, to the right and left of the **Estrada Monumental**, which runs westwards, is the sprawl of the hotel zone of Funchal, where the waterfront houses enjoy exclusive access to the coast. The ocean only becomes freely accessible to the public again where the old lido used to be, which was destroyed by storms in February 2010. The **marine promenade** begins here and passes newer hotel complexes as far as Praia Formosa, and from there on to Câmara de Lobos. The new section includes a seabridge that reaches far into the water

Reid's Palace

AROUND FUNCHAL

Roughly 4km/2.5mi northeast of the town centre there are marvellous views from the botanical gardens. Until 1936, the estate belonged to the Reid family, the English hoteliers. Since 1952 it has been the municipal property of Funchal. Closely resembling a park, the garden has three delightful viewing points and showcases both **indigenous and imported plants**, palms, orchids, bromeliads, succulents and useful or medicinal plants. Some places within the grounds look a little neglected. The former manor house contains a small, old-fashioned museum of natural history which, in addition to a simple yet highly informative exhibition about Madeira's flora and fauna, including stuffed animals and specimens of plants, also has a collection of fossils found on the island.

Colourful parrots from all over the world inhabit the spacious aviaries of the **Loiro Parque** (tropical bird park) below the botanical gardens.

A **cable car** connects the botanical gardens to ▶Monte. Covering a distance of some 1600m/5250ft, the journey takes around 14 minutes and affords splendid panoramic views across the bay of Funchal. The cable car crosses the Ribeira de João Gomes valley with its ancient laurel woods, ending in Monte at Largo das Babosas, close to the famous pilgrimage church.

*Jardim Botânico e Loiro Parque

❶ daily 9am – 6pm, admission: €3, free admission on March 21 (World Forest Day), on April 30 (Garden Birthday), on May (World Museum Day), on July 1 (Madeira's Autonomy Day) as well as September 27 (World Tourism Day)

In Jardim Orquídea on Rua Pita da Silva, below the bird park all types of **orchids** are displayed, from seeds to blossoming plants. A mini

Jardim Orquídea

Quinta do Palheiro

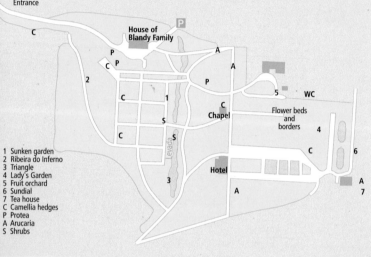

Entrance

C

House of Blandy Family

P

P P C

2

C 1

S

C

S

Chapel C

A

A

P

5 WC

Flower beds and borders

4

A

C 6

Hotel

3

A

A 7

1 Sunken garden
2 Ribeira do Inferno
3 Triangle
4 Lady's Garden
5 Fruit orchard
6 Sundial
7 Tea house
C Camellia hedges
P Protea
A Arucaria
S Shrubs

café in the garden is a nice place to take a break and enjoy the lovely view

Quinta da Boavista on Rua Lombo da Boa Vista offers another beautiful collection of orchids and a wonderful garden.

❶ **Jardim Orquídea:** daily 9am – 6pm, admission: €5, www.madeiraorchid. com

Quinta da Boavista: Mon – Sat 9am – 5.30pm, admission: €3.50, www. madeira-tourist.com/leisure/quinta-da-boavista.html

Quinta do Palheiro (Blandy's Garden) Approximately 10km/6mi northeast of Funchal, not far from the road to Camacha, the rambling grounds of the Quinta do Palheiro, **one of the most beautiful parks on Madeira, are open to the public.

In 1790, the Conde de Carvalhal engaged a French landscape gardener to design the 12ha/30-acre estate. His first residence, now a hotel, stands in the lower part of the park. The atmosphere of the 37-room accommodation is luxurious and cultivated. Golfer who use the Palheiro golf course also like to stay here. One of the count's nephews later redesigned the park in the style of an English garden – the result is a remarkably harmonious **alliance of English and**

Quinta do Palheiro is one of the most beautiful manor houses on Madeira

French horticulture. In 1885, the Blandy family acquired the park and erected a new building in the upper half. The variety of plants in the gardens has to be seen to be believed. Many are extremely rare. The finest time to explore the gardens of the Quinta do Palheiro is when the camellias are in bloom, between December and May; however, they are also famed for their lilies of the Nile, magnolias and proteas, the latter introduced by Mildred Blandy from her South African homeland. Some araucaria and decorative conifers can be seen beneath the trees. In times gone by, the frogs in the ponds were primarily destined for the count's dinner table.

Insider Tip

❶ 9am – 4.30pm, admission: €10.50, www.palheirogardens.com, www. casa-velha.com

In the north of Funchal lies the Parque Ecológico do Funchal (10 sq km/2.4 acres; ▶p. 171). It extends from the riverbed of the Ribeira Santa Luzia up to the heights of the Pico do Arieiro. The nature park was established in 1994 and includes picnic areas, signposted hiking and walking paths, montainbike trails, geocoaching points and opportunities for canyoning (Ribeira das Cales / Chão da Lagoa).

Parque Ecológico do Funchal

* Jardim do Mar

✦ C 2

Altitude: 0 – 175m/574ft
Population: 250

The idyllic alleyways of the fishing village of Jardim do Mar, the »garden of the sea«, should be reconnoitred on foot. The alleys are in part paved with pretty mosaics.

The church of **Nossa Senhora do Rosário** stands on the main square; the church building was financed by emigrants from the village and energetically supported by the remaining inhabitants. The painted rosette is said to have been inspired by that of Notre-Dame in Paris. A small street runs down to the sea, past a picturesquely situated cemetery and the ruins of a sugarcane factory to the »portinho«, or mini harbour. An **ostentatious promenade** runs along the coast and a small bathing area has been made.

Paúl do Mar is one of the most unaltered villages on Madeira

For the sports-minded: Jardim do Mar is **popular with local surfers** on account of the powerful breakers. Large numbers of water sports enthusiasts can be seen at Ponta Jardim, one of the three pebble beaches of Jardim do Mar.

AROUND JARDIM DO MAR

Moving northeast, via a 3km/2mi long tunnel, Paúl do Mar is the next coastal settlement after Jardim do Mar. The village follows a long, narrow road along the bank and is **unique and unspoilt in character**. The atmosphere in the old part of Paúl do Mar makes it unique among the villages on Madeira.

Paúl do Mar

Two bars (one with a restaurant) offer diversion in the small fishing harbour; other localities are in the newer part of the village, further to the west, where emigrants returning from overseas reside in villas. A promenade has also been constructed here. The old centre has been upgraded with a bathing area and a fishing sculpture. On the other hand, the fish market hall has had to go.

High above Paúl do Mar, Prazeres sits on a ridge amongst fruit trees and vegetable gardens, a good **place to begin a hike through the lovely scenery** of western Madeira. Well worth seeing are the paved square in front of the church and the Quinta Pedagógica; the parish priest started this plant and animal garden with a small tea house and production of marmalade, apple wine and herbal teas.

Prazeres

Steep ancient connecting tracks between Jardim do Mar and Prazeres, at a height of 600m/1970ft, are used today mostly by hikers.

Jardim do Mar

WHERE TO EAT
Joe's Bar €
Vereda da Igreja, 12
tel. 2 91 82 22 42
Rustic bar with a tiny garden and a few hearty meals like frango piri-piri (spicy chicken).

WHERE TO STAY
Paúl do Mar ApartHotel €€
Ribeira das Galinhas, Paúl do Mar
tel. 2 91 72 42 29
www.hotelpauldomar.com
House located in a quiet area at the end of the village; the owner values ecological care. There are 60 generous rooms with a view of the ocean, a swimming pool and bike rental.

Hotel Jardim do Mar €
Sítio da Piedade
Jardim do Mar
tel. 2 91 82 22 00
www.hoteljardimdomar.com
Family-run, longstanding house with a terrace restaurant in the middle of Jardim do Mar, but with a view of the ocean.

✳ Machico

✦ C 7

Altitude: 0 – 150m/490ft
Population: 11,500

The fishing harbour of Machico, on the estuary of the little river bearing the same name, is Madeira's second-largest town, with some 12,000 inhabitants. Here, on an easily accessible stretch of coast, João Gonçalves Zarco is thought to have landed in 1419, setting foot on Madeira for the first time.

Madeira's first settlement

Not long after Zarco arrived, the first settlement was established. Under Tristão Vaz Teixeira, Machico actually became the main town in the eastern part of the island from 1440. However, when Funchal became the sole capital of Madeira in 1497, Machico's significance waned rapidly – the action shifted to the new centre on the south coast.

Due to countless attacks by pirates between the 15th and 17th centuries, no less than three forts were built. The place is said to be named

Machico

N ↑   100 m
©BAEDEKER

Rua do Senhor dos Milagres
Ribeira de Machico
Rua da Estacada
Largo dos Milagres
Capela dos Milagres
Rua de Leiria
Nossa Senhora da Conceição
Câmara Municipal
BANDA D'ALÉM
R. Conselheiro J.R. Cunha
Praia de Machico
Forte de São João Baptista
Monumento do Tristão Vaz Teixeira
R. d' Amargua
R. d. Mercado
Rua do Infante D. Henrique
Rua da Árvore
❷
❶
Praceta 25 de Abril
❶
Praceta 25 de Abril
Forte de Nossa Senhora do Amparo
Baia de Zarco
Praia de Machico
Canical
VR 1
Oceano Atlântico
Praia de São Roque
❷
Capela de São Roque
Santa Cruz, Funchal

Where to eat ❶ Mercado Velho
❷ O Goncalves

Where to stay ❶ White Waters Hotel
❷ Residencial Família

after Robert Machyn, who according to legend was shipwrecked here with his lover Anne Dorset (▶MARCO POLO Insight, p. 166).

WHAT TO SEE IN MACHICO

The real centre of Machico is the old town, situated on the west bank of the river Machico. The parish church of **Nossa Senhora da Conceição** (Our Lady of the Immaculate Conception, late 15th century) is also here. Both of the portals from the age of Manuel I are intact, as is the arch of the Vaz Teixeira family mausoleum. The altars with gilded wood carvings and the painted wooden ceiling date back to the Baroque era. There is a monument commemorating Tristão Vaz Teixeira on the square next to the church.

Old Town

In the **Solar do Ribeirinho**, a 17th century patrician house with a beautiful garden, there is a small museum. Four thematic areas bring the local people and stories of more than six centuries to life.

Walk from the pretty town hall towards the sea to get to the new market hall. The old triangular **harbour fortress Forte Nossa Senhora do Amparo** from the 17th century stands watches over both sides of the bay. Today it houses a tourist office.

Solar do Ribeirinho: Rua do Ribeirinho, 15, Tue – Fri 10am – 12.30pm and 2pm – 5.30pm, Sat 10am – 1pm, admission: €1.50, tel. 2 91 96 41 18

Machico

INFORMATION
in the Forte Nossa Senhora do Amparo
tel. 2 91 96 22 89

WHERE TO EAT
❶ *Mercado Velho* €€
Rua General António Teixeira Aguiar
tel. 2 91 96 59 26
A wonderful little place with a terrace under high trees, well suited for a break.

❷ *O Gonçalves* € – €€
Rua do Ribeirinho, 1
tel. 2 91 96 66 06
Fresh fish, grilled or in soup, warm apple cake – in a contemporary setting, as Madeirans love it.

WHERE TO STAY
❶ *White Waters Hotel* €€
Praceta 25 de Abril
tel. 2 91 96 93 80
www.hotelwhitewaters.com
Modern straightforward hotel with 19 rooms between the beach and the town centre. A good restaurant is attached.

❷ *Residencial Família* €
Sítio Pé da Ladeira
Caminho de São Roque, 23/24
tel. 2 91 96 94 40
www.residencial-familia.com
Family-run bed & breakfast on the western edge of town offers 9 rooms with balconies and solid, dark wood furniture; good breakfast.

A Debatable Discovery

1419 is the year noted in history books for the conquest of Madeira – but when was the archipelago actually discovered? A sea chart dated 1351 already plots the island in the Atlantic. More mysterious by far is the legend that a pair of English lovers discovered Madeira.

The two Portuguese captains, **João Gonçalves Zarco** and **Tristão Vaz Teixeira**, commissioned by Henry the Navigator to explore the oceans, first set eyes on Madeira in 1418 – having been blown off course, so the story goes – when they landed on the uninhabited island of Porto Santo. A second expedition took them to Madeira. They took some time to pluck up the courage to set foot on the larger island. Above all, the dramatic cloud cover which sometimes hung over the landscape led Zarco to believe that this could indeed be the »Mouth of Hell«.

Sea Chart of 1351

The Madeiran archipelago was first plotted on a Florentine nautical chart as early as 1351. Madeira is marked as »I. do lolegname«, which may be derived from the Arabic »el aghnam«, meaning »**wood island**«. Porto Santo (»Porto Séo«) and the Ilhas Desertas (»I. deserte«) are also represented. It is

Only an approximate location of the Atlantic islands can be found on old globes.

a matter of speculation whether Italian sailors who regularly made their way to the Canaries, Arab seamen or even Phoenicians, Carthaginians or Romans were aware of the archipelago.

The Legend of Robert Machyn and Anne Dorset

When historical questions remain open, the scope for myths is great. The best-known and perhaps the most intriguing legend relates that the English nobleman **Sir Robert Machyn** (or Machin) who, in 1346 – five years before Madeira appeared on the sea chart mentioned above – was exiled from his homeland for an undisclosed offence. Accompanied by his lover, a certain **Anne Dorset**, who was apparently below his social rank, he set out for Portugal. A storm dragged his ship off course, forcing him to land on Madeira in the bay where **Machico** now stands – its name derived from the Englishman's own, so the legend would have us believe. Machyn and a servant reconnoitred the island. When they returned after three days, ship and crew had vanished. Only Anne remained, but she died a few days later. Robert buried her under a wooden cross and built a chapel in her memory. He and his servant then constructed a boat, set sail and landed on the coast of Africa – at the exact same point where his renegade comrades, captured by Moors, were now stranded. Cast into the same dungeons as his crew, Robert furiously set upon the

This monument in Funchal commemorates the discoverer Zarco

traitors. The King of Fez heard the story, thus learning of the existence of Madeira. However, neither the Moorish ruler nor the Castilian monarch to whom Robert was dispatched showed any interest in the uninhabited island.

Variations on a Theme

There are numerous variations on the legend of Madeira's discovery. Some depict Anne as a noble lady and Robert as a lowly knight. One particularly touching version has Zarco, aware of the lovers' tragic fate, finding the wooden cross which marked the spot where Anne and Robert were buried – both having perished on the island in this account. The crew, the narrative goes on, had etched their story into the cross, concluding with a request: should Christians ever happen to find the spot on the island, they should erect a chapel here. Zarco respected their pious wish and built a small house of worship, which was then completely destroyed by a flood in 1803.

Baroque radiance in the parish church Nossa Senhora da Conceição

A fortress once stood beyond the promenade in front of the Forum de Machico (with a cinema, restaurant and sunbathing terrace) at the southwestern edge of the bay, since replaced by the Hotel Dom Pedro. The **Capela de São Roque** to its rear is sadly closed more often than it is open. It was erected in 1489 following a plague epidemic, with a fountain from a source believed to have miraculous properties. Some remarkable **azulejos** – scenes from the life of Saint Roch – also merit closer inspection.

On the eastern side of the harbour bay, the **old fishing district** of Banda d'Além stretches as far as the Forte São João Baptista (1800). An artificial beach with **light sand** was made here and a beach promenade was constructed.

The **Capela dos Milagres** is located in the centre of the fishing village on Largo dos Milagres. Apparently Zarco had a chapel built here around 1420 on the tomb of Robert Machyn and Anne Dorset, some say. Others claim that a Franciscan monk said mass here for the first time on Madeira on 2 July 1419. The original chapel was destroyed by floods in 1803, but the crucifix, washed away into the ocean, was discovered some days later by fishermen out at sea. This story is well illustrated in a naive painting inside the church, which was rebuilt in 1815. In honour of the figure of Christ, considered miraculous ever since, a supplicatory procession is held on 8 and 9 October.

AROUND MACHICO

*Pico do Facho
Northeast of Machico, the Pico do Facho (literally, peak of the torch) rises up. It earned its name by virtue of its role as a sentinel post entrusted with lighting great bonfires to forewarn the inhabitants of Machico of impending pirate attacks.

Miradouro Francisco Álvares de Nóbrega
At the southwestern entrance to the town of Machico, the Miradouro Francisco Álvares de Nóbrega, named after one of Madeira's most important poets (1773 – 1807), provides a marvellous view of the bay of Machico and the ▶Ponta de São Lourenço.

✶✶ Monte

✦ **C 6**

Altitude: approx. 450 – 600m/1450 – 1950ft
Population: 6700

In the 19th century and up to the 1940s, Monte was a popular climatic spa for wealthy Madeirans and foreigners. Numerous grand houses and villas along with some very fine hotels, graced with lush tropical gardens, testify to earlier days of tourism.

As tourists gravitated towards the coastal areas around Funchal, the status of Monte, some 8km/5mi higher up from the capital, declined. The idyllic **Largo da Fonte** (fountain square) is a reminder of former glories, with the former rack railway station and the marble chapel of Capelinha da Fonte.

Just in front, leaving the main street, a steep climb up to the right leads to the restored **Quinta Jardims do Imperador**, the final residence of Karl I of Austria (▶Famous People), with beautiful gardens and a tea pavilion.

Climatic spa with tradition

❶ Caminho do Pico, Mon – Sat 9.30am – 5.30pm, admission: €6

The journey to Monte itself is quite an experience, if the **cable car** (Teleférico) from Funchal is the chosen form of transport for the ascent. Looking out of the gondolas, there are splendid views of Funchal and the surrounding landscape. One way of getting back down is a basket sled (▶MARCO POLO Tip). From 1893, a **rack railway** ran between Terreiro da Luta, a short distance north of Monte, and Funchal. A steam boiler exploded in 1919, causing four fatalities and many serious injuries. Presumably this was the reason for public use of this means of conveyance declining rapidly. A road had also been built meanwhile. The rack railway was decommissioned in 1939.

✶✶Teleférico and basket sleds

MARCO ⊕ POLO TIP

! *Sledding in the middle of summer*

It's definitely not cheap fun but the basket sled ride from Monte down to Livramento (about €25 €/2 pers.) should be part of every Madeira programme. Two drivers run next to this unique means of transport to steer and brake.

Insider Tip

WHAT TO SEE IN MONTE

Close to the Monte cable car station, point of departure for Funchal's botanical gardens, the pilgrimage church of Nossa Senhora do Monte stands over the heart of the village. 68 steps lead up to it. Its façade,

✶Nossa Senhora do Monte

The sarcophagus of Karl I, the last Austrian emperor, is kept in the pilgrimage church Nossa Senhora do Monte

set off with dark tuff and flanked by a pair of towers, can be seen from afar. The previous church was destroyed by the earthquake of 1748 and rebuilt in Baroque style in 1818. The **view** from the church terrace across Funchal bay to Cabo Girão is marvellous. All that is left of the original chapel is a Pietà, set in silver, in the high altar. This figure of the Virgin Mary is revered by the local population as the miraculous **patron saint of the island** and carried through the alleyways of the town in a grand procession (Romaria) every year on 15 August (Assumption Day). In the left side chapel, the plain **sarcophagus** contains the mortal remains of the last Austrian Emperor **Karl I** (►Famous People).

**Jardim Tropical Monte Palace

Below the church of Monte, the Jardim Tropical Monte Palace lies in the grounds of the former Grand Hotel Belmonte – now owned by the Berardo Foundation for culture art, technology and science – and is open to visitors. In this imaginatively landscaped park an **abundance of art objects** can be admired, including many azulejos detailing the history of Portugal, a tiled walkway featuring works from the 15th to the 20th century, the world's largest hand-thrown vase,

Monte

WHERE TO EAT
Restaurante Monte Garden
€€ – €€€
Caminho do Monte, 192
tel. 2 91 72 42 36
Quinta do Monte has a stylish restaurant with an à-la-carte menu. The café pavilion serves light meals or just a cup of tea with a view of Funchal.

Café do Parque €   Insider Tip
Am Largo da Fonte
tel. 2 91 78 28 80
The Café do Parque serves local cuisine under beautiful, tall trees.

WHERE TO STAY
Quinta do Monte €€€
Caminho do Monte, 192
tel. 2 91 72 42 36
www.quintadomontemadeira.com
All 51 rooms and suites of the magnificent quinta, which is located in a beautiful park, are furnished very comfortably.

FESTIVAL
The high point of the religious festivals on Madeira is the big pilgrimage to Monte on August 15 (Assumption of the Virgin). The pilgrimage church Nossa Senhora do Monte is then decorated beautifully.

according to the Guinness Book of Records, over 5m/16ft tall and weighing 550kg/1210lb, an oriental garden, exhibitions of porcelain and a small mineralogical museum.
❶ daily 9am to 5pm, museum daily 10am to 4.30pm, admission: €10, www.montepalace.com

Parque Ecológico do Funchal
The entrance to the Parque Ecológico do Funchal, the ecology park, can be found at the Riberia das Cales forest guard's lodge on the road from Monte to the Poiso Pass. On both sides of the well-maintained hiking trails, largely indigenous vegetation and tree species can be seen, as along a narrow **panoramic road**. This is a cul-de-sac, hence the same route has to be followed back.
❶ daily 9am – 6pm, free admission, info tel. 2 91 78 47 00

Terreiro da Luta
In Terreiro da Luta, about 3km/2mi north of Monte, close to the former rack railway station a 5.5m/18ft-high and about 20 t in weight statue of **Nossa Senhora da Paz** (Our Lady of Peace) stands in a marvellously scenic location. Her story goes as follows: in the First World War, a German submarine fired at and sank the French warship Surprise in the bay of Funchal. The Madeirans then vowed to erect a monument to the Virgin Mary after the conclusion of the war. By 1927, enough donations had been collected to honour the promise, with the former Empress of Austria, Zita, one of the notable benefactors. A highly **unusual rosary**, crafted from the anchor chain of the sunken ship, is wound around the plinth.

** Paúl da Serra

───────────✦ **B / C 3 / 4**

Altitude: 1300 – 1400m/4225 – 4550ft
Location: 60km/38mi northwest of Funchal

The plateau of Paúl da Serra covers an area of around 102 sq km/39 sq mi and is thus Madeira's only plain of note.

Barren plateau

This **barren region, reminiscent of the Scottish Highlands** with its abundance of sheep and goats living in the wild, forms a stark contrast to the picturesque blossoms seen elsewhere in the varied landscapes of Madeira and is a paradise for hikers. The highest peak is Ruivo do Paúl (1640m/5380ft). Above a mountain hut maintained by the island government, there is a vantage point on the Bica da Cana (1620m/5314ft) to the east.

The Paúl da Serra Plateau (translated, mountain moor) plays an **important role in the island's water supply**. Its porous rock behaves

The wide, well-watered plateau Paúl da Serra is reminiscent of Scottish Highlands

like an enormous sponge, soaking up precipitation. The water either flows into streams or one of the many levadas which begin their journey into the valleys here (►MARCO POLO Insight, p. 174). A distinctive feature of the Paúl da Serra landscape since 1993 has been the appearance of **wind turbines**.

ENCUMEADA PASS

The Encumeada Pass is situated at a height of 1004m/3290ft, east of the plateau at the intersection of the 110, which runs across the Paúl da Serra, and the old mountain road, the 228. The 228 was the only connection by road between São Vicente on the north coast and Ribeira Brava on the south coast before the tunnels were completed. On a clear day, the vantage point presents excellent **views of the mountainous landscape** and **the ocean beyond the north and south coasts**.

**Vantage point

RABAÇAL

Rabaçal (1064m/3490ft) lies in a striking valley cutting at the western end of the plateau and basically consists of a few deserted inns. The name means something like »untouched«. The surroundings are truly breathtaking, richly forested with ancient laurel and tree heath, interspersed with a wide variety of ferns, moss and lichen.
The area around Rabaçal is a very **popular destination for weekenders** who can enjoy any of a number of delightful picnic areas. An old lane which leads down to Rabaçal has been closed to traffic, so hikers have to leave their vehicles in the unsecured car park on the

Paúl da Serra

WHERE TO EAT
Pastor do Paúl €€
Pico da Urze
tel. 2 91 82 01 50
http://hotelpicodaurze.com
There are only two places to eat in the isolated mountain region. This one serves everything from plates of ham through salads down to rabbit – and of course there are the traditional Madeira specialities as well.

WHERE TO STAY
Pousada dos Vinháticos € – €€
Serra d'Água
tel. 2 91 72 42 72
www.pousadadosvinhaticos.com
Flowered curtains, comfortable chairs, one of the two hotel buildings has walls made of wooden beams – this pousada with 21 nicely furnished rooms, a restaurant and a small terrace for eating snacks is located not far from the Encumeada Pass.

Madeira's Levadas

There is enough water on Madeira, but only in the north. So the first Portuguese settlers had to come up with a way to irrigate their terraced fields in the south of the island. They transported it in stone channels, the levadas.

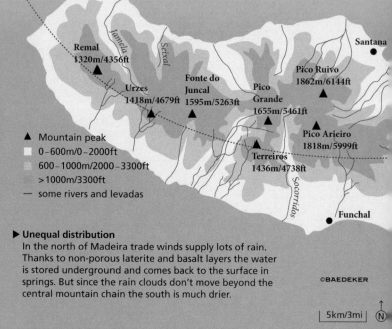

Remal
1320m/4356ft

Santana

Urzes
1418m/4679ft

Fonte do
Juncal
1595m/5263ft

Pico Ruivo
1862m/6144ft

Pico
Grande
1655m/5461ft

Pico Arieiro
1818m/5999ft

Terreiros
1436m/4738ft

Funchal

▲ Mountain peak
☐ 0–600m/0–2000ft
☐ 600–1000m/2000–3300ft
☐ >1000m/3300ft
— some rivers and levadas

©BAEDEKER

| 5km/3mi | Ⓝ

▶ **Unequal distribution**
In the north of Madeira trade winds supply lots of rain. Thanks to non-porous laterite and basalt layers the water is stored underground and comes back to the surface in springs. But since the rain clouds don't move beyond the central mountain chain the south is much drier.

▶ **Levadas**
The stone channels are just one meter (3 feet) wide and half a meter deep. 200 levadas were counted at the beginning of the 19th century. In 1966 the last levada, Levada dos Tornos, was built. It is 106km/636mi long and runs through 16km/10mi of tunnels, of which the longest is 5.1km/3mi long. The water that is transported through Levada dos Tornos irrigates 9900ha/24,750acres of land.

▶ **Precipitation per year**

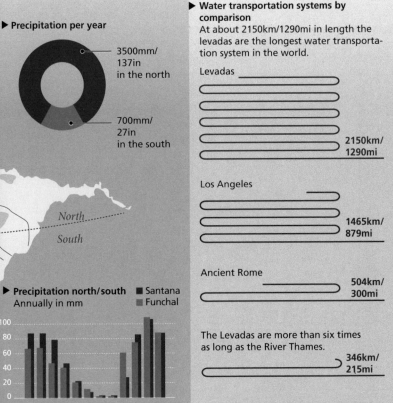

3500mm/
137in
in the north

700mm/
27in
in the south

North

South

▶ **Precipitation north/south**
Annually in mm

■ Santana
■ Funchal

▶ **Water transportation systems by comparison**
At about 2150km/1290mi in length the levadas are the longest water transportation system in the world.

Levadas

2150km/
1290mi

Los Angeles

1465km/
879mi

Ancient Rome

504km/
300mi

The Levadas are more than six times as long as the River Thames.

346km/
215mi

Many of the narrow and shallow levadas are interconnected. They must be maintained constantly, for which small paths have been made alongside of them. These are now popular hiking trails.

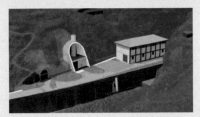

▶ **Hydropower plants**
The hydropower plant Socorridos works along similar lines. It is fed via a 15.5km/9mi-long tunnel and canal system and supplies the region Funchal/Câmara de Lobos with electricity and water.

Water is for Everyone

One of man's greatest achievements on the island of Madeira is the elaborate irrigation system of canals, totalling some 2150km/1335mi in length. Construction of the levadas, as they are called, began around the time that the first settlers arrived on Madeira.

Madeira's first settlers were confronted with the **problem of even distribution of water**: frequent rainfall in the damp north meant that this part of the island had more than enough, whereas the much sunnier south was prone to aridity.

It is not known who initiated the construction of the levadas – from the Portuguese »levar«, meaning »to lead« – but what is certain is that slaves from Africa and La Gomera, one of the Canary Islands, dug the first channels. The **island's**

Very popular among tourists: hiking along the levadas

topography presented the most difficult obstacle, with every stone, every tool having to be carried to the most favourable route for the levada. Labourers often found themselves suspended between heaven and earth, as well as having to lower their equipment down steep rock faces by rope. Most of the levadas were actually created in the 20th century, such as the Levada dos Tornos above Funchal, through which water flowed for the first time in 1966. Measuring over 100km/60mi with approximately 100,000 outlets, it supplies water to more than 10,000 ha/24,700 acres of agricultural land.

Water and Power

The levadas today still draw water from natural springs and large reservoirs which ensure that the water flows evenly. Before reaching the fields, the water has already served one other useful purpose, namely as a power supply. A more efficient harnessing of this energy source can barely be conceived.

Levada Law

To facilitate a fair distribution of water to farmers and peasants, levada law was established in the early years and remains largely intact today. **Levadeiros** keep the complex canal system running smoothly and oversee water distri-

The footpaths next to the levadas were intended for maintenance workers, not for hiking

bution. Anyone who has a legitimate interest is entitled to the amount required. Landowners are thus obliged to offer up any water source within their territory for general consumption. In return, the government does not charge for water from the levadas and pays for their upkeep.

Hiking Trails

As time passes, the levadas have become more and more of a tourist attraction. The pathways alongside the canals, originally constructed for **maintenance workers**, have found favour with hikers.

Not every levada trail is suitable for a hike, however. Some should only be attempted by those with a head for heights or with experience of mountainous terrain. These paths often run along rock faces with no protection from a sheer, vertical drop and are so narrow that it is just about possible to place one foot in front of the other. Fainthearted readers take note!

There are also less strenuous trails, however, and whatever your level of fitness, levada hikes are a splendid way to discover Madeira's beautiful landscape.

plateau and start the worthwhile descent into the valley from here. No public transportation runs to Rabaçal. Anyone who wants to explore the valley alone should get there early – either with a rental car or a taxi. Alternatively, almost all of the local tour agencies offer a hiking trip to Rabaçal.

The most popular walks

A challenging hike, best left well alone by vertigo sufferers, is the trail from Rabaçal to the **»25 Fontes«** (»25 springs«), taking around 2 hours. Here a number of gushing streams flow in small cataracts into a mere which, depending on the time of year, may or may not be full. The water of this decidedly picturesque little lake feeds the Levada do Risco. An easier hike, half an hour in duration, follows this particular levada to the Risco waterfalls, which boast some of Madeira's most spectacular cataracts in the wetter months of the year.

Insider Tip

The path for both hikes commences at the former car park in Rabaçal. After some 200m/200yd natural steps lead down to the »25 springs« to the right. To reach the waterfalls, continue straight ahead rather than following the steps.

** Pico Ruivo · Pico do Arieiro

✴ B/C 5

Location: Central Madeira

Madeira's highest peak

North of Funchal are Madeira's highest mountains, the Pico Ruivo (1862m/6100ft), the Pico das Torres (1851m/6070ft) and the Pico do Arieiro (1818m/5960ft). In the late morning, cloud cover often impairs the view, so it is advisable to set off early in the day.

Above the clouds

Pico Ruivo is Madeira's highest mountain. Even when the lower reaches of the island are shrouded in thick mist, its rugged, ruddy peaks can often still be seen in clear sunshine – the hike to the top reveals how varied the Madeiran weather can be.

Pico do Arieiro is the third-highest mountain on the island – and at the same time **the most easily accessible**. A decent road ends just a few metres below the summit, bringing Funchal within an hour's reach. The final, 7km/4mi stretch of road, branching off at Paso de Poiso, initially passes through dense woodland which gives way to increasingly open heathland before arriving in rocky, cragged mountain terrain with breathtaking views. A number of vantage points along this road provide magnificent views of Madeira, provided the weather remains fair. A radar station on the plateau at the summit spoils the fantastic panorama. A simple path leads down to the **Mi-**

Resting at Pico do Arieiro with an overwhelming view

radouro do **Juncal** viewpoint (1800m/5905ft), where there is a panorama of Madeira's northern coast.

The hike from Pico do Arieiro to Pico Ruivo takes around four hours and is extremely worthwhile, but requires **stamina and sound equipment**. The magnificent panorama of the entire island from the summit is more than ample reward for such efforts.

**From Pico do Arieiro to Pico Ruivo

* Ponta Delgada

 **B 5**

Altitude: approx. 10 – 165m/32 – 541ft
Population: 1300

The small town of Ponta Delgada on the north coast of Madeira boasts a popular seawater swimming pool. Powerful breakers constantly replenish the basin with fresh water from the ocean.

Ponta Delgada

WHERE TO EAT
Solar de Boaventura €€ **Insider Tip**
Sítio do Serrão
tel. 2 91 86 08 88
www.solar-boaventura.com
Cultivated restaurant in Boaventura,
which occasionally serves game. Good
accommodations also available.

WHERE TO STAY
Monte Mar Palace Hotel €€ – €€€
Sítio do Montado
Ponta Delgada
tel. 2 91 86 00 30
www.montemarpalace.com

Comfortable house right on the coast
105 spacious rooms, some with an
ocean view. Relax at the beautiful pool
or in the sauna. There is a golf training
course.

Casa da Capelinha €€
Sítio do Terreiro
tel. 2 91 86 00 40
www.casadacapelinha.com
Quiet, historic hotel with an additional
modern house. Only twelve rooms in all,
all of them with a balcony/terrace or
garden.

Picturesque pilgrimage site

Fruit and vegetable cultivation are of economic significance here,
whilst much of the osier used in Madeiran basketry also grows here.
In and around Ponta Delgada there is a noticeably large number of
quintas, built by the grand winegrowers who accumulated their riches in the 18th century. Down by the sea is the old heart of the town,
with the new town higher up on the other side of the through road,
which was improved by adding a tunnel – 2400m/7900ft long and the
drive to São Vicente is two or three minutes shorter.

WHAT TO SEE IN AND AROUND PONTA DELGADA

*Capela do Bom Jesus

Every year in Ponta Delgada, on the first Sunday in September, **one
of the oldest religious festivals** on Madeira takes place. The occasion relates to a legend from the year 1470, when a chest containing
a wooden crucifix was washed up on the shore – just as a small chapel was about to be built there, thus earning it the name of Capela do
Bom Jesus. In 1908 the pilgrimage church completely burned down.
Nothing survived, save for the charred remnants of the cross, preserved since then in a glass case inside the new church (1919) and
revered by the religious local population. The **unusual fresco adorning the church ceiling** is striking: it includes depictions of paradise
and a ship of the Knights of Christ, symbolizing the Portuguese discoveries. The beautifully located rest home close to the church was
originally a pilgrim hostel.

South-east of Ponta Delgada, the coastal road leaves the ocean and after 2km/just over a mile reaches **Boaventura** (1500 inhabitants), nestled between fruit gardens and sprawling **osier plantations for local basket weaving**. The basis of this region's fertility is the plentiful water supply, as a number of small rivers originating in the central mountains flow through here on their way to the Atlantic. Boaventura itself has little in the way of sights, but is ideal for relaxing in lovely surroundings. Many visitors to the island see Boaventura as an ideal starting point for attractive hikes.

Boaventura

** Ponta de São Lourenço

C 8/9

Altitude: 0 – 322m/1056ft
Location: 34km/21mi east of Funchal

Raw cliffs, coarse vegetation and a predominantly stiff, head-on breeze – this is the east of Madeira, a fascinating contrast to the lush greenery which thrives elsewhere on the island.

At the craggy eastern point of Madeira, Ponta de São Lourenço, the vulcanic origins of the island can be seen clearly

Madeira's eastern peninsula	Ponta de São Lourenço has more in common with Porto Santo than Madeira in terms of sparse vegetation. It can be reached via a road tunnel, 750m/800yd in length, at ▶Caniçal. The road ends at a car park, high above Abra Bay, with a view into the distance over a **near-vertical drop and rugged rock formations** along the coast. To the northeast, the neighbouring island of ▶Porto Santo can be seen, to the southeast the Ilhas Desertas. The stratification of some of the cliffs of Ponta de São Lourenço provides a compelling insight into the volcanic origins of the island.

Numerous wind turbines generate energy for the industrial and free trade zone of Caniçal.

Accessible only on foot Starting at the car park, a rewarding hike (around 4 hours there and back) to the hut **Casa da Sardinha** on a trail that is in part secured by wooden railings; in two places it is possible to go down to the sea.

Ilhéu do Farol, Ilhéu de Agostinho Off the coast of Ponta do Furado lie the deserted islands of Ilhéu de Agostinho and Ilhéu do Farol, the latter with a lighthouse erected in 1870 which marks the **easternmost point of Madeira**.

Ponta do Pargo

✴ B 1 ●

Altitude: 473m/1550ft
Population: 1100

The sleepy village of Ponta do Pargo is Madeira's western-most settlement and scene of an annual apple festival in September. All imaginable manifestations of the fruit are celebrated. The terraced fields here are wider and less steep so that tractors can be deployed on the fields – practically unique on Madeira!

Westernmost point of Madeira New construction — a motorway, a large nursing home and a golf course — have made great changes in the former farming community. Ponta do Pargo boasts **Portugal's highest lighthouse** (392m/1286ft), crowned in bright red paint. It is situated around 1.5km/1mi outside the village at the westernmost point of Madeira, signalling to ships the safest route around the island and presenting fine views of the west. But the building craze has left its mark here as well: in 2011 the 273m/900ft-long Tunel do Farol was built to lead to the lighthouse.

Equally worthwhile is the view from the **miradouro**, a viewing point about 1km/0.5mi away.

Ponta do Pargo

WHERE TO EAT
Casa de Chá »O Fio« € – €€
Rua do Fio – Salão de Baixo
tel. 2 91 88 25 25
Modern atmosphere behind rustic stone walls at the observation point. Local cooking, good cake.

O Farolim € – €€
Rua Dr. Augusto França, 66
tel. 2 91 88 21 42
The restaurant serves some unusual creations made of local products; worth a try.

In the late 1990s, the small church of Ponta do Pargo, dedicated to Saint Peter, was enhanced with an unusually **colourful ceiling fresco** featuring paradisiacal landscapes.
Lighthouse: daily 9.30am – 12noon and 2pm – 4.30pm

At Achadas da Cruz there is a spectacular observation point, a cable car (teleférico) runs almost vertically down the cliff.

Achadas da Cruz

✳ Ponta do Sol   ✦ C 3

Altitude: approx. 30 – 180m/100 – 590ft
Population: approx. 4200

Ponta do Sol was home to the grandfather of the US author John Roderigo dos Passos (1896 – 1970), who found international fame with *The 42nd Parallel* and *Manhattan Transfer*.

Ponta do Sol, on the south coast of Madeira, was founded as early as 1450, granted its town charter in 1501 and was, for many years, a centre of sugarcane cultivation. Today, sugarcane has given way to **banana plantations**. Produce from one of Madeira`s biggest banana packing plants is transported from the town, its by lorry to Funchal before leaving the country on export.

Bananas, poets and tourists

The grandfather of **John dos Passos** emigrated to the USA in the 19th century. His grandson visited his ancestor's homeland on a number of occasions, the last visit being in 1960. A commemorative plaque can be seen on the former family home in Rua Príncipe D. Luís I, more recently converted into a **cultural**

! *Levada route*   **Insider Tip**

MARCO ⊕ POLO TIP

A short but quite steep wooden ladder and a winding path connect the two levadas in ther valley of Ponta do Sol. This makes one of the few circular hiking routes on Madeira possible.

Afternoon sun over Ponta do Sol

centre. Ponta do Sol's ambitions of becoming a more lively tourist destination have only been partially realized, although the place is a popular port of call for almost every organized tour of the island. In addition to its picturesque seafront promenade and a small, grey pebble beach, it offers a restful and relaxed environment.

WHAT TO SEE IN PONTA DO SOL

Picturesque townscape Arriving from Ribeira Brava, the finest view of this picturesque little town, flanked by high rock faces, can be enjoyed from above it on the road which meanders its way into the valley. The inviting alleyways and steps between the houses, bedecked with flowers, are perfect for a leisurely stroll.

*Nossa Senhora da Luz The church of Nossa Senhora da Luz (Our Lady of the Light) stands on the site of an earlier structure from the 15th century. Tangible relics from the original church are confined to a statue of the patron saint and a baptismal font said to have been donated by King Manuel I himself. The present church was renovated in the 18th century in colourful, intricate Baroque style. The **original wooden Mudéjar ceiling** was retained in the chancel, albeit repainted in the style of the day.

Quinta de João Esmeraldo Just 2km/about a mile higher up, in the district of Lombada, the Quinta de João Esmeraldo stands at the heart of extensive banana plantations. In the 15th century its landlord, a **companion of Chris-**

Ponta do Sol

WHERE TO EAT
Poente € – €€
Cais da Ponta do Sol
tel. 2 91 97 35 79
Located above the beach at Ponta do Sol, the Poente is known for good fish dishes.

WHERE TO SLEEP
Estalagem da Ponta do Sol **Insider Tip**
€€€ – €€€€
Caminho do Passo, 6
tel. 2 91 97 02 00
www.pontadosol.com
Modern hotel flooded with light, on a rock above Ponta do Sol. All 54 rooms have a balcony, some with a fantastic ocean view. Relax in the infinity pool or in the wellness area with sauna, whirl-pool or a massage. Enjoy the great view of the ocean while eating in the restaurant as well.

Hotel da Vila €€
Rua Dr. João Augusto Teixeira
tel. 2 91 97 33 56
www.pontadosol.com; 16 rooms
Sister house of the boutique hotel Estalagem on the cliff; its facilities are also available For guests of the Vila. Lots of white, wood and local materials.

SHOPPING
»Adega da Vila« in Ponta Sol Shopping, Estrada do 5 Centenário, offers a great selection of Madeira and other Portuguese wines.

topher **Columbus**, ran one of Madeira's largest sugarcane plantations with hundreds of slaves. The pink mansion, also said to have been frequented by Christopher Columbus, now belongs to the regional government and serves as a school.

Opposite, the **Espírito Santo** chapel features beautiful wood carvings and azulejos.

** Porto Moniz   ✵ A 2/3

Altitude: approx. 10 – 280m/30 – 900ft
Population: 1700

The coastal road winds its way from the west in countless twists and turns down to the ocean and Porto Moniz, at the northwesternmost point of the island. There are beautiful views of the coastal village already when approaching it.

The little town has long been a popular summer resort for tourists and Madeirans alike, not least because it has the only campgrounds on the island; its infrastructure has developed considerably and the **Popular summer resort** new coastal promenade bears witness to a modernization programme. **Wine growing** complements tourism as an important economic factor.

The town's name honours the Portuguese nobleman Francisco Moniz, who settled here in 1533. Thanks to an outcrop of rock that juts far out into the ocean and the Ilhéu Mole, complete with lighthouse, Porto Moniz is the best-protected harbour on Madeira's northern coast and was a whaling station for many years.

WHAT TO SEE IN PORTO MONIZ

**Lava swimming pools

Insider Tip

Amongst the most popular attractions are the **natural swimming pools of lava rock** which have formed along the deeply fissured coast. The surf ensures that the water is constantly renewed, as waves wash over into the basin. There is a small entrance fee for the Piscinas Naturais seawater pools, but changing rooms, lounging areas and a snack bar are on hand.

Porto Moniz

INFORMATION
Rotunda da Piscina
tel. 2 91 85 25 55, 2 91 85 01 93

WHERE TO EAT
Pérola do Norte € – €€
Rua do Ilhéu Mole
tel. 2 91 85 30 00
Pleasant family restaurant; the grilled fish is especially good.

A Latada €
Sítio da Pedra Mole
This simple street bar is located above the town; it serves hearty snacks (for example, innards), and sometimes there is a daily special like fish with beans. There is a small terrace for seating.

WHERE TO STAY
Hotel Moniz Sol €€
Rua Forte de São João Batista, 7
tel. 2 91 85 01 50

www.hotelmonizsol.com
The Moniz Sol with 45 rooms is the largest hotel in town. Comforts include a heated indoor pool and a sauna; there is a diving school next door. The hotel also offers boat tours.

Pensão Salgueiro € – €€
Lugar do Tenente, 34
tel. 2 91 72 42 80
www.pensaosalgueiro.com
Family-run bed & breakfast with 18 in part spacious rooms (with kitchenette); many rooms have an ocean view. A popular restaurant is attached to the bed & breakfast.

MARKET
»Feira de Porto Moniz«, an agricultural exhibit with various sales booths, espetada booths and a cattle market, is held every year in July.

The new centre for life sciences is situated on the coastal promenade, featuring temporary exhibitions – fascinating for children too. **Centro de Ciência Viva**

❶ Tue – Sun 10am – 7pm, admission: €5, www.portomoniz.cienciaviva.pt

Parts of the old São João Baptista fort, which protected the settlement from pirates in days gone by, have been reconstructed at the harbour and a small aquarium, **Aquário da Madeira**, was established. A helipad has also been built, along with ample mooring berths for yachts. **Harbour**

❶ **Aquário da Madeira:** daily 10am – 6pm, admission: €7

AROUND PORTO MONIZ

Ribeira da Janela (population 230) lies southeast of Porto Moniz on the river of the same name, which leaves its deep valley bed here as it flows into the sea. Three rock formations rise up from the water here, one of which, the Ilhéu da Ribeira da Janela, gave the place and the river their names on account of a **naturally occurring opening, shaped like a window** (in Portuguese: *janela* = window). The village itself, higher up the valley at a height of 450m/1475ft, is well worth a visit. Its lofty location and attractive townscape are matched by **marvellous scenery** in the surrounding area. A little-used road winds its way up to the Paúl da Serra plateau. ***Ribeira da Janela**

Ribeira da Janela played an important role in the construction of **hydroelectric power stations** in a programme initiated during the Salazar dictatorship in the 1970s. Today, Madeira has four such hydropower stations, although they account for only a relatively modest share of the island's electricity. Part of the island's energy supply is now generated by wind turbines.

Swimming fun at Piscinas Naturais in Porto Moniz

** **Porto Santo**

⸺ ✦ **E – F 10/11**

Altitude: 0 – 517m/1696ft
Population: 5500
Location: 43km/26mi northeast of the main island of Madeira

Porto Santois also known as the »golden island«. The lush vegetation which makes Madeira so attractive is absent here, but Porto Santo does have something in abundance which is virtually nonexistent on Madeira: turquoise-coloured water and a splendid, golden-yellow sandy beach, some 9km/5.5mi in length and said to be healthy, although there is no real scientific evidence to support the claim.

Five small, rocky islands surround the island of Porto Santo, which lies 43km/27mi northeast of Madeira. Roughly 11km/6.5mi long and approx. 6km/3.5mi wide, Porto Santo has an area of 42.5 sq km/17 sq mi, its highest point being Pico do Facho at 517m/1703ft. Of the once

What Madeira doesn't have, Porto Santo has at a length of 9km/5mi: sand beaches, which are supposed to have healing powers

numerous mineral springs, from which water was once bottled for export, most have dried up. Earlier, limestone was mined on Ilhéu de Baixo off the coast to the south, then fired on Porto Santo and sold as fertilizer or mortar to Madeira. The people on Porto Santo currently earn their living mainly from **tourism**, some from **fishing and making wine**. There is also an airport, constructed by NATO in 1960.

The beautiful sandy beach on the south coast and good infrastructure have led to a constant increase in tourism in recent years. During the summer holidays, Porto Santo is particularly popular with Madeiran families. The even climate means it is possible to swim in the sea at any time of year. There is a thalassotherapy centre in Cabeço, south of the main city. The newest attraction is a golf course in the south, between Capela de São Pedro and the north coast.

**Homely holiday island

Porto Santo

ARRIVAL
Ships run daily between Madeira and Porto Santo (duration: about 2 hours). The small turboprop airplanes are quicker; they take off several times a day from Santa Catarina Airport (flying time: about 20 min.).

INFORMATION
Av. Henrique Vieira e Castro
tel. 2 91 98 51 89

SPORTS
Not just swimming is popular on Porto Santo; sailing, surfing, riding and biking are also possible.

WHERE TO EAT
Vila Alencastre €€ – €€€
on the ER 111, Campo de Baixo
(opposite Supermarkt Zarco)
tel. 2 91 98 50 72
Down to earth Portuguese cooking is served on a green patio.

Bar João do Cabeço € – €€
Cabeço da Ponta

tel. 2 91 98 21 37
Snackbar with a small selection of good, inexpensive home cooking (for example, meat rolls); free WLAN after 6pm.

WHERE TO STAY
Hôtel Porto Santo & Spa
€€€ – €€€€
Campo de Baixo
tel. 2 91 98 01 40
www.hotelportosanto.com
The hotel has 97 rooms and five apartments in an attractive modern design. The spa offers sauna, hamam, steam bath, heated indoor seawater pool as well as sand therapy in a copper tub.

Hotel Torre Praia €€ – €€€
Rua Goulart Medeiros
Vila Baleira
tel. 2 91 98 04 50
www.portosantohotels.com
66 rooms and suites
The modern hotel is on the beach in Vila Baleira. Relax by the swimming pool and on the sun terrace with an ocean view.

Reforestation   Porto Santo was once densely covered with dracaena, junipers and heather. The first settlers cleared the fertile land to cultivate grain, earmarked for Portuguese expeditions overseas, a lucrative business. However, the land soon karstified and the earth was washed away by rainwater. Grain cultivation revived in the 18th century, as evidenced by windmills in the landscape.

Today, there is relatively little in the way of cultivation of grain, grapes, fruit or vegetables, but efforts are being made to return the terrain to its verdant state through intensive reforestation.

History   João Gonçalves Zarco and Tristão Vaz Teixeira sought out the archipelago in 1418 and first explored the more easily accessible Porto Santo (»Holy Harbour«). In 1419, they returned with Bartolomeu

Porto Santo

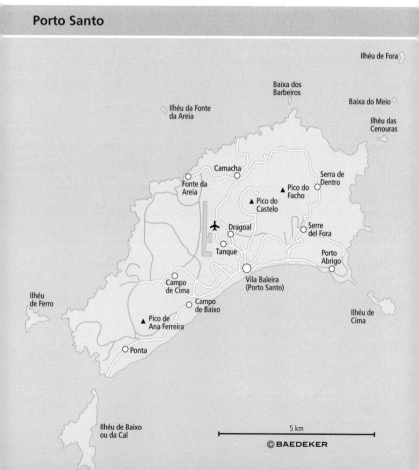

Perestrelo, who set about cultivating the land with the aid of Portuguese settlers.

Porto Santo's most celebrated inhabitant was **Christopher Columbus** (►Famous People), who is thought to have spent a number of years on the island around 1450 with his wife Filipa Moniz, Perestrelo's daughter. In the 16th and 17th centuries pirate raids became such a concern that the islanders erected fortifications and, on occasion, seriously considered moving across to Madeira.

> **?** MARCO ● POLO INSIGHT
>
> *Medieval rabbit plague*
>
> In the annals of Porto Santo, it is written that a pregnant rabbit that was released into the wild in 1418 had so many offspring that the ensuing overpopulation became a real problem for newly arriving settlers.

WHAT TO SEE ON PORTO SANTO

The **main settlement and harbour**, Vila Baleira, formerly Porto Santo, is situated on the flat south coast of the island. This modest town has an unhurried air, in spite of being home to the majority of Porto Santo's population. It contains a market hall, a handful of small hotels and restaurants. The market hall, which is now only used as a cafeteria stands almost on the seafront, whilst a craft centre (Centro de Artesania) featuring various shops is located on Rua Manuel Gregório Pestana jun. Vila Baleira

The main square of Vila Baleira is the beautifully paved **Largo do Pelourinho**, meeting point for locals and tourists. »Pelourinho« means pillory, and one stands in the square as a symbol of jurisdiction. The plain white parish church of **Nossa Senhora da Piedade** was rebuilt after it was pillaged by pirates in 1667. Its most attractive feature is the azulejo of a Pietà which graces the outer wall. The **town hall** (Câmara Municipal), a fine architectural example of Portuguese Renaissance architecture, also stands on Largo do Pelourinho.

An appealing little museum in the **Casa Museu Cristóvão Colombo**, where Columbus is purported to have lived, displays all manner of artefacts from daily life, marine charts, documents and depictions of the history of seafaring and the like.

❶ Tue – Sat 10am – 12.30pm, 2pm – 5.30pm, Sun 10am – 1pm, July – Sept until 7pm, admission: €2

OTHER PLACES ON PORTO SANTO

On the road from Vila Baleira heading northeast, the small church of Nossa Senhora da Graça was constructed in 1951 on the site of a chapel dating back to the 15th century. It is venerated on account of Nossa Senhora da Graça

Casa Museu Cristovão Colombo, once possibly the home of
Christopher Columbus, is now a museum

a miraculous mineral spring. The island's most important religious
festival is held here annually on 15 August (Feast of the Assumption).

Portela
viewpoint
From the Portela viewpoint further to the east, fine views across the
south and east of Porto Santo, with the small island of Ilhéu de Cima
and its lighthouse, can be enjoyed.

Pico do
Castelo
North of Porto Santo rises the tree-covered Pico do Castelo
(437m/1433ft), an extinct volcano, cone-like in shape. At the summit,
the scant remains of a 16th-century fortress still stand. There is a
monument to the instigator of the reforestation efforts. In Camacha,
north of the Pico do Castelo **traditional wine is produced** – these
days with up-to-date methods. The wine can be sampled here.
Beyond Camacha on the north coast, the waters of the **Fonte da**
Areia are said to help alleviate stomach, bowel and skin ailments.
Some consider it to be a veritable fountain of youth. Those who are
simply hungry or thirsty can stop off for a picnic.

Pico de Ana Ferreira (283m/928ft) in the western part of the island features interesting **formations of basalt columns**. The simple **Capela de São Pedro** (17th/18th century), which only opens its doors to the public on St Peter's Day (29 June), is perched on its southern face. Golfers will be pleased to find an 18-hole course close by.

MARCO POLO TIP

! *Comfortable or keen* Insider Tip

The coastal bike path on Porto Santo is ten kilometers (six miles) long, flat the whole way and runs parallel to the golden sand beach. Anyone keen for more can bike around the island – with three respectable inclines.

From Ponta da Calheta, a popular swimming spot at the **southwestern tip of Porto Santo**, there are marvellous views of Ilhéu de Baixo off the coast and, on a clear day, Madeira and the Ilhas Desertas. Restaurants in the vicinity serve exquisite fish dishes.

Ponta da Calheta

✳ Ribeira Brava

— ✦ C 4

Altitude: approx. 30 – 180m/98 – 590ft
Population: 6600

Ribeira Brava came to prominence as the point at which the north-south axis across the Encumeada Pass and an east-west trading route intersected.

Ribeira Brava, an erstwhile fishing village at the mouth of the wild watercourse of the same name, lies on Madeira's southwest coast. In the summer months little more than a glorified rill, winter rainfall can see it swell rapidly to a raging torrent – hence the name »**wild river**«. As the communications infrastructure improved, the village enjoyed a certain degree of prosperity, developing into a favoured weekend destination amongst the local population. As a consequence, numerous apartment houses have sprung up behind the old centre. These can be bypassed by tunnel, whilst a wide, attractive promenade with sweeping open spaces has been constructed on the seafront. A further attraction is the pebble beach that is protected by a jetty on the western side of town with a small pool and permanent sun umbrellas.

»Wild river«

WHAT TO SEE IN RIBEIRA BRAVA

A walk through Ribeira Brava is enough to see a number of handsome examples of typical Madeiran architecture: colourful window

Spruce townscape

Ribeira Brava

INFORMATION
in the Forte de São Bento
tel. 2 91 95 16 75

WHERE TO EAT
Restaurante Borda D'Água
€ – €€
Rua Engenheiro Pereira Ribeiro
tel. 2 91 95 76 97
www.restaurantebordagua.ondebiz.com
Bright, modern beach restaurant with a
large selection of fish dishes and snacks.

Restaurant & Grill Muralha **€€**
Estrada regional 220, 1
tel. 2 91 95 25 92
In the colourful eatery with terrace
above the beach on the road meat and
fish specialities as well as cocktails are
served.

WHERE TO STAY
Quinta do Cabouço **€€**
Caminho do Cabouço
tel. 9 18 69 69 96
www.quintadocabouco.com
Restored, charmingly decorated 18th
cent. manor house with a large garden
in a quiet panoramic location above the
main town. There is room for up to 8
people (self-catering), dinner can be
booked for weekends.

FESTIVAL
Insider Tip
Every year on June 29 the
town holds a huge festival in honour of
St Peter with a boat procession as the
high point as well as many booths and
stands, many right at the beach.

shutters, wrought-iron balcony railings and fine façades. The remains
of an old fort, constructed in the 17th century to guard against cor-
sair raids, can be seen on the river promenade. Today, the tourist information office is located here.

Igreja de São Bento On an ornately paved square in the centre stands the Igreja de São
Bento, a pretty village church from the 16th century, its **tower covered with blue and white tiles** and crowned with an armillary
sphere. The font is thought to have been donated by King Manuel I
in 1500. Also worthy of inspection are a Manueline pulpit, splendid
Baroque altars and a number of elaborate azulejos. Valuable Flemish
paintings can be seen on the sides of the chancel.

Townhall Just a few steps from the church, Ribeira Brava's town hall, a well-
preserved **mansion** built in 1776, stands amidst beautiful, park-like
gardens, ideal for a break.

Museu Etnográfico Those interested in the history of Madeira should pay a visit to the
modern museum of ethnography (Museo Etnográfico). The layout
is both interesting and entertaining, offering an insight into Madeiran fishing, the Madeiran countryside, viniculture and cooperage,

as well as much worth knowing about the weaving trade; old basket sleds and oxcarts are also on display. Appealing craftwork is sold in the museum shop.

❶ Rua de São Francisco, 24, Tue – Sun 10am – 12.30pm and 2pm – 6pm, admission: €2.50

✳ Ribeiro Frio

✦ C 6

Altitude: 860m/2821ft
Population: 100

At the heart of a mountain landscape and the last uninterrupted area of laurisilva forest on the island, the small settlement of Ribeiro Frio – »cold river« in translation – tends to be rather busy at times. All the bus tours on the island converge here to visit the trout farms which have been set up on the initiative of the state.

WHAT TO SEE IN RIBEIRO FRIO

Trout are bred in basins arranged in terraces and supplied with oxygen-rich water from the Ribeiro Frio river. The fish are sold to caterers and restaurants or cast into the wild streams of the island for anglers to catch. The trout farming station at Ribeiro Frio is a pleasure for all the senses: the basins are integrated into a quaint little park with fragrant box hedges.

*Trout farming

Behind Victor's Bar lies the **Parque Florestal das Queimadas**, a nature reserve and **UNESCO World Heritage site** since 1999, intended to protect the virgin **laurisilva forest** which has survived. Many endemic species of plants growing here are also to be safeguarded against extinction.

Ribeiro Frio

WHAT TO EAT
Victor's Bar € – €€
tel. 2 91 57 58 98
Rustic excursion restaurant, which serves delicious fresh trout (Port. truta).

From Ribeiro Frio, a hiking trail which follows the Levada do Furado comes complete with the considerable reward of the viewing point at Balcões. The simple hike lasts for something like one hour (there and back) and passes through splendid scenery on its way to the viewing point, with marvellous views of the highest peaks on Madeira – Pico Ruivo, Pico das Torres and Pico do Arieiro. Those who feel fit enough,

*A hike to the Balcões viewing point

Insider Tip

Visiting the Ribeiro Frio trout farm includes strolling through a beautiful park with tree ferns

have a head for heights and are steady on their feet can walk in the opposite direction along the Levada do Furado as far as Portela.

★ Santa Cruz

✦ **C 7**

Altitude: 0 – 150m/490ft
Population: 6000

The town on the south coast of Madeira has remained largely unchanged and due to its proximity to Santa Catarina Airport, this delightful place is barely on the tourist radar.

Waterfront stroll
A beautifully paved waterfront promenade, lined with palm trees, is an inviting setting for a stroll. The pebble beach, with its colourful fishing boats and shady palm trees, is also as pretty as a picture. At

the edge of town, the popular **Praia das Palmeiras** beach attracts bathers. Another beach area has been developed to the west near the Santa Cruz yacht club.

WHAT TO SEE IN SANTA CRUZ

The quaint and narrow alleyways of the old town lend it a strikingly homogeneous appearance. The 16th-century town hall, embellished with Manueline stonemasonry, is worthy of note. Close to the church, the courthouse with its curved flight of steps also merits a look. Having grown rich on the profits of sugarcane cultivation, the community built itself **Madeira's second-largest church after the Sé in Funchal**. The parish church of São Salvador was constructed in 1533 on the remains of an older chapel. A tomb dating back to 1470 is a survivor of the original building. The sacristy contains 16th-century azulejos that once graced the walls of Nossa Senhora da Piedade, the Franciscan monastery that gave way to the airport. Evidence of Manueline style can be found in a window and a portal in the choir.

*Homogeneous ensemble

Two tile pictures by the Portuguese artist António Aragão (1921 – 2008) with fishing and planting themes decorate the façade of the old market hall. The hall is supposed to be used for cultural purposes in the future.

Market hall

Santa Cruz

WHERE TO EAT
Restaurante Praia das Palmeiras
€€
at the beach
Rua Praia Palmeiras
tel. 2 91 52 42 48
The tasty fish dishes served here are just the thing after a day at the beach. Seating is on the terrace.

WHERE TO STAY
Quinta Albatroz Beach & Yacht Club **€€€ – €€€€**
Quinta Dr. Américo Durão
Sítio da Terça
tel. 2 91 52 02 90

www.albatrozhotel.com
The 20 large rooms all have a view of the ocean and a balcony or terrace. There are fresh and salt water swimming pools, a beautiful garden and a good restaurant.

Hotel Vila Galé **€€ – €€€**
Rua de São Fernando 5
tel. 2 17 90 76 17
www.vilagale.com
Most of the 262 rooms have an ocean view; there is a beautiful pool landscape with palm trees and a view of the Atlantic and a generous fitness area.

✳ Santana

✦ **B 6**

Altitude: 420m/1377ft
Population: 3500

At the heart of Madeira's most fertile region lies Santana. Surrounded by floral splendour, Santana's beautiful thatched houses make the town one of the most picturesque places on the island. Sanatan and the area were named UNESCO biosphere reserve in 2011.

WHAT TO SEE IN AND AROUND SANTANA

The traditional Casas de Colmo (straw houses) are listed buildings, their **triangular straw roofs extending down to the ground** to protect the interior from the ravages of the weather. Today, there are far fewer of these houses, which have little room under their expensive and high-maintenance roofs.
The local council has erected two such houses as models alongside the town hall – one of which serves as the tourist information office.

*Casas de Colmo

An interesting place to visit in Santana is the **theme park for the history and culture of Madeira** (Parque Temático da Madeira). Four pavilions focus on, among other things, the island's discovery and the future of our planet. A water mill, ox-drawn sleds, a hedge labyrinth and a small lake with boats are also on offer. The 7 ha/17-acre site also boasts a replica of the historic Monte rack railway train. Two restaurants and a bar keep hunger at bay.
❶ daily 10am – 7pm, admission €10, www.parquetematicodamadeira.pt

Madeira yesterday, today and tomorrow

In March 2012 a small biosphere garden was opened in the town after the district was made a UNESCO biosphere reserve. It is representative of the numerous endemic species of fauna and flora in the archipelago's major ecosystems.

Biosphere garden

From the outskirts of Santa, a cable car (teleférico) leads down the steep coastline to Rocha do Navio (Sat, Sun, Wed; exact timetable available from the tourist information office in Santana). The beach below is not particularly inviting, but the journey reveals spectacular scenery.
❶ Wed, Sat, Sun, the tourist information office in Santana has the exact opening times

Cable car to Rocha do Navio

Steep gables and thatch are characteristic of the famous Casas de Colmo in Santana

Santana

INFORMATION
Sítio do Serrado
tel. 2 91 57 29 92

FESTIVALS
Santana is famous for its folklore festival »48 Horas de Bailar«, which takes place in the middle of July; right at the beginning of the month »Mostra Gastronômica« also offers culinary specialities along with music and dance.

MARKET
Insider Tip
A farmer's market, where flowers, vegetables, fruit and honey are sold, is held every Sunday from 10am on the road to Pico Ruivo.

WHERE TO EAT
Quinta do Furão €€€
Achada do Gramacho
tel. 2 91 57 01 00
www.quintadofurao.com
North of Santana on the coast with a beautiful view of the sea. Excellent cooking in a quite unique setting. A modern hotel is attached to the house.

Cantinho da Serra €€
Estrada do Pico das Pedras
tel. 2 91 57 37 27
Baby goat in a pot, stockfish from the oven, lamb and other local specialities in a somewhat up-market value, served in a former manor house at the edge of town (towards Pico das Pedras).

Restaurante Serra e Mar €
Sítio da Igreja
tel. 2 91 57 46 80
Simple snack bar below the church towards the teleférico (cable car station); the menu includes pork with chouriço, clams or a seafood stew.

WHERE TO STAY
O Colmo €€
Sítio do Serrado
tel. 2 91 57 02 90
www.hotelocolmo.pt
Quite pleasant hotel with 43 rooms and suites in the centre of Santana. It has an indoor pool, a sauna, a fitness area as well as a bar and a good restaurant.

*Excursion to the Casa das Queimadas
A pleasant excursion from Santana leads to the Casa das Queimadas (883m/2896ft), a forest ranger lodge with picnic areas in the mountains southwest of Santana. Continuing south, hikers arrive at the lush **Parque Florestal das Queimadas** on the slopes of Pico Ruivo (1862m/6108ft), whose summit can be reached from here.

✳ Santo da Serra

✦ C 7

Altitude: 675m/2214ft
Population: approx. 1600

Santo da Serra – Santo António da Serra, to give it its full name – is situated on a meadowy plateau in eastern Madeira. It has long been valued as an up-market climatic spa.

The rich merchant families of Funchal favoured the area, particularly in the 18th century, as the ideal place to build their quintas. Today, Santo da Serra is best known for the spectacular scenery of its golf course (▶p. 101, 103).

Insider Tip

WHAT TO SEE IN SANTO DA SERRA

Gardens close to the church in the centre of the village that originally belonged to the grounds of the Quinta do Santo da Serra have been remodelled as a public park. Today they are **popular among Madeirans and foreign visitors**. Agapanthus, camellias and hydrangeas line a very beautiful path through the pretty park, which features a number of playgrounds and sports fields, as well as a small deer park.
The quinta once belonged to the Blandy family; their old summer house is hidden behind hedges and tall trees.

*Quinta do Santo da Serra

Santo da Serra

WHERE TO EAT
A Nossa Aldeia €€
Caminho do Arrebentão
Sítio dos Casais Próximos
tel. 2 91 55 21 42
Simple, hearty food is served here, like skewers (espetadas), stockfish and lamb.

WHERE TO STAY
Quinta do Pântano €€
Estrada da Fonte
de Sto. António, 61

tel. 9 64 00 69 07
www.quintadopantano.com
Two studios and a house for four people on the grounds of a country quinta with a pond and animals. Breakfast is made with organic products from the quinta.

MARKET
On Sunday from 12noon near the church the »Feira da Ladra«; with vegetables, fruit, clothing and much more.

*Miradouro dos Ingleses From the Miradouro dos Ingleses (viewpoint of the English), hewn out of the rock in the lower part of the park, it is possible to look east as far as ▶Machico and the ▶Ponta de São Lourenço peninsula.

The miradouro earned its name by virtue of the English merchants who stationed a look-out here. When the person on watch relayed news of a trading vessel spotted on the horizon, enterprising businessmen still had enough time to hurry to Funchal in time for the docking and unloading of the ship.

✳ São Jorge

✳ B 6

Altitude: approx. 10 – 150m/32 – 492ft
Population: 1500

In and around São Jorge on Madeira's northern coast grow many of the osiers which are used in basketry and also play a major role in viniculture.

WHAT TO SEE IN AND AROUND SÃO JORGE

*Igreja de São Jorge In São Jorge stands one of the island's most remarkable churches, certainly the most beautiful of its kind on the north coast. **Dedicated to Saint George, the Baroque church** was erected on a hill to replace a 15th-century chapel that was destroyed by floods in 1660. Whilst the exterior is unostentatiously plain – a typical example of Madeiran understatement in religious architecture – the interior of the church is richly decorated with gilded woodcarvings, beautiful altarpieces and supremely artistic azulejos.

São Jorge

WHERE TO EAT
Casa de Palha €
Achada Grande, (behind the church)
tel. 2 91 57 63 82
This unique eatery in a traditional wooden house serves simple snacks.

WHERE TO STAY
Quinta da Quebrada €€
Caminho Municipal da Furna
Sítio da Quebrada

Arco de S. Jorge
tel. 2 91 57 01 80
mobile 9 67 97 55 43
www.quintadaquebrada.com
On the grounds of the quinta in a lush green garden on the slope to the coast nine small houses are rented. They vary greatly in style and size; furnishings are simple and neat. Some have a view of the sea. Breakfast is included.

Ponta de São Jorge with its lighthouse offers fantastic views of both the east and west coast, as it reaches far out into the ocean.

*Ponta de São Jorge

Between São Jorge and Arco de São Jorge to the west, also off the beaten track, lies the Cabanas viewing point. This is one of the most breathtaking panoramas of the north coast. Fruit stalls of local farms and a souvenir shop attract visitors. The fact that almost every tourist coach stops here has brought a certain amount of bustle, but São Jorge now enjoys a modest prosperity.

*Miradouro Cabanas

In the **Quinta do Arco** in Arco de São Jorge the former mayor of Funchal and his wife had an opulent public rose garden planted with more than 1700 plants.

Rosarium

Insider Tip

❶ April – Dec daily 10am – 6pm, admission: €5, www.quintadoarco.com

✱✱ São Vicente

✦ B 4

Altitude: approx. 15 – 350m/49 – 1148ft
Population: 3200

São Vicente is a convenient starting point for the ascent of the Pico dos Tanquinhos (1524m/5000ft) and Ruivo do Paúl (1640m/5380ft), which provides splendid views across the mountains.

The attractive north coast town is located on the estuary of the Ribeira de São Vicente. A few hotels and restaurants have been built in recent times right on the coast, but the town itself can be found a little further inland surrounded by high mountains and sheltered behind a slope – a prudent strategy to avoid the attention of pirates. In 1928, parts of São Vicente were buried by a landslide.

WHAT TO SEE IN SÃO VICENTE

Altogether, São Vicente presents a harmonious appearance, not least because its inhabitants collectively took responsibility for the appearance of their houses and renovated them in the 1980s. The reward was – as was the purpose of the exercise – a **conservation award** and rising numbers of visitors.

*Picturesque townscape

The Baroque parish church, built in the 17th century, merits closer inspection. Gilded wood carvings and paintings adorn the interior, with the image of Saint Vincent adorning the ceiling.

*Igreja de São Vicente

São Vicente

WHERE TO EAT
Taberna de São Vicente €€
Sítio do Calhau
tel. 2 91 84 80 34
Berto and Zeta have collected ideas from all over Portugal and serve everything from octopus to steak.

WHERE TO STAY
Quinta Estalagem do Vale €€ – €€€
Sítio da Feiteira de Baixo
tel. 2 91 84 01 60
www.estalagemdovale.com
After an exciting history this historic manor house, which is located about two kilometers/a good mile above the town, was converted into a hotel with 40 modestly furnished rooms. There is also a restaurant and a bar.

Quinta Casa da Piedade €€
Sítio do Laranjal
tel. 2 91 84 60 42
www.casadapiedade.com
The pretty quinta in a well-tended garden offers seven attractively and nicely furnished rooms.

The Grutas de São Vicente were formed when streams of lava flowed down from the mountains into the valley 890,000 years ago

The paved square in front of the church depicts the **attributes of São Vicente**: two ravens who defended the saint's corpse and the unmanned ship from which his body was washed ashore, as legend would have it, on the south coast of Portugal.

At the point where the Ribeira de São Vicente flows into the Atlantic, a striking rock formation reaches upwards, its summit cross visible from far out to sea. Constructed in the year 1692, the small Capela de São Roque features interesting pebble mosaics on the façade facing inland.

Capela de São Roque

The caves of São Vicente were only opened to the public in 1996, though they were discovered much earlier. A guided tour through the imaginatively illuminated caves lasts for roughly one hour and resembles a **journey to the interior of the earth**. The caves were formed by mighty lava streams which flowed downwards from the ▶Paúl da Serra region some 890,000 years ago, when Madeira's volcanoes erupted for the last time, lending the island its definitive topographical character.

*Grutas de São Vicente

The Volcanism Centre gives interesting insight into the subject. A garden of predominantly indigenous plants has also been created.

Insider Tip

❶ daily 10am – 6pm, admission: €8, www.grutasecentrodovulcanismo.com

Seixal

✴ **B 3**

Altitude: approx. 10 – 350m/30 – 1148ft
Population: 700

Seixal, charmingly situated on a mountainside jutting out into the ocean, is renowned for its excellent, fragrant Sercial wine. Arduous labour is required to cultivate the vines here.

Roughly halfway between ▶Porto Moniz and ▶São Vicente, nestling among wine terraces on the slopes of a mountain spur, lies the small settlement of Seixal. Waist-high hedges protect the tracts of land from the force of the Atlantic winds.

Surrounded by vines

Seixal is approached on the VR2 from the east. A tunnel goes around the village itself, so watch for the turn-off. Once one of the most impressive stretches of the northern coast road ran along here. A new road VR2 (Via Rapida) now runs parallel to this narrower, older road that and passes through numerous tunnels, cutting the journey time. But the old route is breathtakingly beautiful. Cut into the almost vertical cliff face, using every technical means possible and no little in-

**Coast road

Seixal

WHERE TO EAT
Casa de Pasto Justiniano €€
Sítio Chão da Ribeira (inland)
tel. 2 91 85 45 59
www.casadepastojustiniano.com
Espetada traditionally served: A laurel
skewer with meat is hung on a chain
above the table; everyone helps himself.
The fresh troutare also delicious.

Brisa Mar €€
Sítio do Cais
tel. 2 91 85 44 76
www.brisa-mar.com
Small, family-run restaurant at the harbour, where good fish has been served
for years – it belongs to the estalagem
of the same name.

WHERE TO STAY
Casa das Videiras €€   Insider Tip
Sítio Serra D'Água
tel. 2 91 22 26 67
www.casa-das-videiras.com
Nice bed & breakfast with only four
small, nostalgically elegant rooms (three
in the main house, which was built in
1867, one in a garden cottage). Casa
das Videiras can also be rented out completely to self-caterers.

Seixal is located on a lava tongue that reaches far into the sea with surf
crashing against its base

genuity, the road passes through narrow tunnels and over stone bridges, immediately above the raging surf. It was used for a long time as a one-way road parallel to the new motorway, but meanwhile rockslides have blocked it in many places. In places where the new road is not running through a tunnel it is still possible to get a small impression of past driving pleasures.

Right on the small harbour in Seixal, where a few fishing boats are still tied up, **sea water swimming pools** have been built that are just as good those in Porto Moniz but less well known. Swim in the quiet waters of the Piscinas Naturais; sanitary facilities and a snack bar are also available. There is a beach at the western edge of town that is very popular among the local people, the **Praia da Laje** set in beautiful landscape.

Swimming

A viewing point around 1km/half a mile east of Seixal has particularly good views of the impressive Véu da Noiva (»bridal veil«) **waterfall**, which cascades down the hillside into the ocean. Liquid refreshment can be obtained at the bar, whilst souvenirs from the shop next door.

*Véu da Noiva

PRACTICAL
INFORMATION

When is the blossoming season on Madeira? What is the best means of transportation on the island? How do I ask for a good restaurant in Portuguese?

Arrival · Before the Journey

GETTING THERE

By air   There are regular air connections between mainland Europe and Madeira. The Portuguese airline TAP has daily **scheduled flights** from London to Madeira: from Gatwick direct to Funchal, and from Heathrow to Funchal via Lisbon. TAP also flies from Lisbon to Porto Santo. In addition, **charter flights** to Madeira are available from a number of British and Irish airports, e.g. Thomson Air from Birmingham, East Midland, Exeter, Glasgow and London Gatwick. Among operators and **budget flights**, Jet-2com flies direct from Leeds and Manchester to Funchal, easyjet direct from Bristol and London Stansted and Gatwick to Funchal.

> **Note**
> Billable service numbers are marked with an asterisk:
> *0180....

The flight time from London to Madeira is approximately three and a half hours. Porto Santo can be reached from Madeira; this flight takes around 15 minutes.

If you have lots of time and a generous budget, there are **two alternatives to flying**: the five-day voyage on a **cargo ship** from Felixstowe to the Madeiran port of Caniçal, returning via the Canary Islands and Cadiz (book through Strand Voyages of London, tel. 020 7921 4340, www.strand-travelltd.co.uk), or the 27-hour **train journey** from London through France and Spain to the Algarve (book through Spanish Rail, tel. 020 7725 7063, www.spanish-rail. co.uk), followed by the 22-hour crossing on the weekly car ferry from Portimão to Madeira (book through Naviera Armas, tel. 00 351 265 546 300, www.navieraarmas.com).

Cruise ships   Madeira is a destination for cruise ships all year round, although most of them only dock at Funchal Harbour for one or two days.

IMMIGRATION AND CUSTOMS REGULATIONS

Travel documents   Travellers from Europe require a valid passport or national identity card. Since 2012 children under the age of 16 must be in possession of their own passport or identity card.

Car papers   A national driving licence usually suffices to rent a vehicle. This should be carried at all times, together with vehicle registration doc-uments and green card (International Motor Insurance Certificate).

AIRLINES
TAP – Air Portugal
In London
tel. 08 45 601 09 32

On Madeira:
tel. 291 239 248 (Funchal airport)
tel. 707 205 700 (Porto Santo)
www.tap.pt

easyjet
tel. 09 05 821 09 05
www.easyjet.com

Jet2
tel. 08 71 226 17 37
www.jet2.com

MADEIRA AIRPORT
Location
approx. 18 km/11 mi east of Funchal

Taxi to Funchal
Journey time approx. 30 minutes, costs between €20 and €30, depend-ing on destination.

Airport bus
Aerobus runs from/to the airport (one-way: €5, return: €7.50; no charge for TAP passengers) and makes 20 stops in all mainly in Funchal and in the hotel zone there up to/from Praia Formosa. Info tel. 2 91 20 11 51

The EU pet pass is necessary to bring in cats, dogs and weasels. The pass must contain the date of the most recent rabies innoculation, which must have been given at least 30 days before entering Madeira and at the most 12 months ago, as well as the identification code of the microchip that has been implanted in the animal, or the animal's tatoo number.

Pets

The states of the European Union form a common economic area, the **European Single Market**, in which the movement of goods for private use is largely exempt from duty. There are certain allowances which travellers from other European countries need to be aware of when arriving in Portugal and Madeira (e.g. a maximum of 800 cigarettes, 10 litre of spirits and 90 litres of wine for visitors over 17 years of age). For travellers from outside the EU, the following duty-free quantities apply: 200 cigarettes or 100 cigarillos or 50 cigars or 250g of tobacco; also 2 litres of wine and 2 litres of sparkling wine or 1 litre of spirits with an alcohol content of more than 22% vol.; 500g of coffee or 200g of coffee extracts, 100g of tea or 40g of tea extract, 50ml of perfume or 0.25 litres of eau de toilette. Gifts up to a value of €175 are also duty-free.

Customs regulations

TRAVEL INSURANCE

Medical care on holiday is provided if a **European Health Insurance Card** (European Health Insurance Card, EHIC) is presented to the

Public health insurance

doctor. This card has now replaced the previous health insurance forms. Even with the card, a portion of the costs of treatment or medicines must, in many cases, be paid for by the patient. On production of the receipts, the outlay will be reimbursed on returning home – although not for every treatment.

Private health insurance   As the patient often has to pay a share of the costs for medical treatment and medicines, and return transport, if necessary, is not covered by public health insurance, an additional private health insurance policy is recommended.

Electricity

On Madeira the mains supply is **220 volts, 50 hertz**. Adaptors are necessary and hard to find on Madeira.

Emergency

EMERGENCY NUMBERS
General emergency number
tel. 112 (calls not charged)

General emergency number
tel. 112
Police, fire brigade, ambulance (calls not charged)

Coastguard
tel. 291 230 112

Emergency doctor for house calls
tel. 2 91 20 44 80

Breakdown service
tel. 800 290 290

Police/Public safety
tel. 2 91 20 84 00

Civil defence
(incl. mountain rescue)
tel. 2 91 70 01 12

Etiquette and Customs

What to wear   As in other southern countries, Madeirans place a lot of value on appropriate clothing. That applies **not only to restaurants in the evening** but also to a shopping or sightseeing trip. Scant leisure clothing is heavily frowned upon for church visits. Men should never be seen bare-chested except on the beach. Women can only go topless at the hotel pool, not on the beach or in public swimming baths.

Gay and Lesbian marriages are allowed in Portugal. Acceptance of gay and Lesbian travellers and locals has definitely grown as well. The »rainbow community« really is much bigger than it seems at first glance. There are no special bars or clubs for gays or Lesbians; most of the larger nightclubs and the established bars are open to homosexuals.

Gays and Lesbians

The Madeirans make a great effort to communicate with their guests in English. However, a few words **of Portuguese** such as »bom dia« (»good morning«) or perhaps to book a room, or order food in a restaurant will certainly be welcomed by the locals as a gesture of politeness to the host country (▶Language).

Bom dia

Health

In Funchal there are several good private clinics as well as public hospitals and the modern Madeira Medical Center; in Caniço there is a polyclinic. The larger hotels often have a designated doctor who can be summoned quickly if the need arises. Otherwise, most places outside Funchal have their own **health centres** (Centro de Saúde), generally with an emergency unit attached. But the staff usually just speaks Portuguese. A visit to the doctor usually has to be paid for right away and the recipt turned in to one's own medical insurance.

Medical care

HOSPITALS IN FUNCHAL

Hospital Cruz de Carvalho
Avenida Luís de Camões
(close to the hotel zone)
tel. 291 705 600

Clínica de Santa Luzia
with 24 hour clinic
Rua da Torrinha, 5
tel. 291 200 000

Clínica da Sé
24 hour clinic
Rua dos Murças, 42
tel. 291 207 676
Some English-speaking doctors and dentists are on call here.

ON PORTO SANTO
Centro de Saúde Porto Santo
Rua Dr. José Diamantino Lima
tel. 291 980 060

Pharmacies

Pharmacies (*farmácias*) can be identified by a green and white sign featuring a cross or snake. All medicines manufactured in Portugal are available here, as well as many international compounds. It may be advisable to bring along any more unusual medicines if these are likely to be needed.

Opening hours for pharmacies are, as a rule, Mon – Fri 9am – 1pm and 3pm – 6pm, Sat 9am – 1pm. Outside these hours, a sign normally indicates the whereabouts of the nearest pharmacy on stand-by duty. If there is only one in the vicinity, the telephone number of a practising pharmacist on emergency duty is also listed.

Information

IN UNITED KINGDOM
Portuguese National Tourist Office
11, Belgrave Square
London, SW1X 8PP
tel. 020 72 01 66 66
tourism.london@portugalglobal.pt
www.visitportugal.com

ATOP (Association of Travel Organisers to Portugal)
Madeira House
High St, Hook Norton
Oxon OX15 5NH
tel. 016 08 73 82 86
www.destination-portugal.co.uk

IN CANADA
Portuguese Tourism Office
60 Bloor Street West Suite 1005
Toronto, ON M4W 3B8
tel. 416 921 73 76
info@visitportugal.com

IN USA
Portuguese Trade and Tourism Office in the USA
590 Fifth Avenue, 3rd Floor
New York, NY 10036

tel. 646 723 0200
www.visitportugal.com

ON MADEIRA
Direcção Regional do Turismo da Madeira
Avenida M. Arriaga, 18
9004-519 Funchal
tel. 00 351 291 211 900
www.visitmadeira.pt

INTERNET
www.acontecemadeira.com
Website in Portuguese with current events on Madeira.

www.visitmadeira.pt
Official tourism website of Madeira, with an English version. General overview on what to see and where to stay on Madeira, highly informative.

www.dnoticias.pt,
http://online.jornaldamadeira.pt
Online version of the two daily newspapers *Diário de Notícias* and *Journal da Madeira* (Portuguese).

www.madeira-web.com
Everything about a Madeira holiday, in English: hotels, weather, walks and pictures from live webcams.

www.madeira-island.com
An English-language guide with hotels, where to shop, information on museums and a list of all festivals on the island.

PORTUGUESE CONSULATES AND EMBASSIES
Consulate in Australia
Level 17, 55 Clarence Street
Sydney N.S.W 2000
tel. 2 926 221 99
mail@cgsyd.dgaccp.pt

Consulate in Canada
438 University Avenue
Suite 1400, 14th Floor
Toronto
tel. 416 217 09 66

Embassy in Ireland
15 Leeson Park, Dublin 6
tel. 1 412 70 40
www.embassyportugal.ie

Embassy in the United Kingdom
11 Belgrave Square
London SW1X 8PP
tel. 020 7235 53 31

Consulate General in the UK
3 Portland Place
London W1B 3HR
tel. 020/ 7291 37 70

Embassy in the USA
2125 Kalorama Road
NW Washington, DC 20008
tel. 202 328 86 10

CONSULATES ON MADEIRA
British Honorary Consulate
Rua da Alfandega, 10, 3C
9000-059 Funchal
tel. 291 212 860
Britcon.Funchal@NetMadeira.com

U.S. Consular Agency
Rua da Alfandega, 10-2F
9000-059 Funchal
tel. 291 123 5626

Language

Portuguese is spoken in Portugal, in Brazil and in the former Portuguese colonies in Africa. On Madeira, English is the most commonly understood foreign language, but it is well worth making the effort to learn at least a few words of Portuguese.

Portuguese and other languages

Most Portuguese words place the emphasis on the penultimate syllable. A general rule is: if a word ends with m, s or the vowels a, e, o, the emphasis is placed on the penultimate syllable. If a word ends with l, r, z or with an ã, i or u, the last syllable is stressed. Accents indicate variations in emphasis. A tilde (~) indicates the nasalization of vowels.

Pronunciation

Portuguese   Portuguese is a Romance language, with early Celtic, Germanic and Arabic influences still present. Written Portuguese is readily identifiable as a Romance language and may be fairly comprehensible to anyone with a grasp of Latin or another Romance language. Spoken Portuguese, on the other hand, is less fathomable: it sounds almost like a Slavic language. It is characterized by soft pronunciation, by syllables that run seamlessly into one another, a proliferation of sibilants and a wealth of differently pronounced vowels. Another feature is the strong emphasis placed on certain syllables, which often leads to the following unstressed syllable virtually disappearing.

Portuguese phrases

At a glance

Yes/no	Sim/Não
Mrs/Mr	Senhora/Senhor
Perhaps	Talvez
Please	Se faz favor
Thank you	Obrigado/Obrigada
You're welcome	De nada/Não tem de quê
Sorry!	Desculpe!/Desculpa!
Okay!	Está bem/De acordo!
When?	Quando?
Where?	Onde?
Excuse me?	Como?
How much?	Quanto?
Where to?	Aonde? Para onde?
What time is it?	Que horas são?
I don't understand.	Não compreendo.
Do you speak English?	Fala inglês?
Please can you help me?	Pode ajudar-me, se faz favor?
I would like …	Queria …
I like it (don't like it).	(Não) Gosto disto.
Do you have …?	Tem …?
What does it cost?	Quanto custa?

Getting acquainted

Good morning /day/evening!	Bom dia!/Boa tarde!/Boa noite!
Hello!	Olá!
How are you?	Como está?/Como vai?
Fine, thank you. And you?	Bem, obrigado/obrigada. E o senhor/a senhora/você/tu?

Goodbye!/See you soon!	Adeus!/Até logo!/Até à próxima!

Finding the way

left/right	ã esquerda/ã direita
straight on	em frente
close/far	perto/longe
Excuse me, where is …?	Se faz favor, onde está …?
How many kilometres is it from here?	Quantos quilómetros são?
I have broken down.	Tenho uma avaria.
Could you tow me to the next garage?	Pode rebocar-me até à oficina mais próxima?
Is there a garage near here?	Há alguma oficina aqui perto?
Excuse me, where is the nearest petrol station?	Se faz favor, onde ésta a bomba de gasolina mais próxima?
I would like … litres …	Se faz favor … litros de …
…Regular petrol/super/diesel.	…gasolina normal/súper/gasóleo.
…Lead-free/ …leaded.	…sem chumbo/com chumbo.
…with …octane.	…com …octanas.
Fill her up, please.	Cheio, se faz favor.
Help!	Socorro!
Watch out! Vorsicht!	Atenção! Cuidado!
Please quickly call …	Chame depressa …
…an ambulance.	…uma ambulância.
…the police/the fire brigade..	…a polícia/os bombeiros.
It was my/your fault.	A culpa foi minha/sua.
Would you give me your name and address, please?	Pode dizer-me o seu nome e o seu endereço, se faz favor?

Eating out

Please could you tell where I can find …	Pode dizer-me, se faz favor, onde há aqui …
…a good restaurant?	…um bom restaurante?
…an inexpensive restaurant?	…um restaurante não muito caro?
…a typical restaurant?	…um restaurante típico?
Is there a bar here/a café?	Há aqui um bar/um café?
Could you please reserve a table for four persons for this evening?	Pode reservar-nos para hoje à noite uma mesa para quatro pessoas, se faz favor?
Could you please give me a …?	Pode-me dar …, se faz favor?
Knife/fork/spoon	faca/garfo/colher
Glass/plate	copo/prato
Pepper	pimenta
Salt	sal

Cheers!	À sua saúde!
Could we pay, please!	A conta, se faz favor.
Did you enjoy your meal?	Estava bom?
The meal was excellent.	A comida estava êcelente.

Sopas, Entradas/Soups, starters

Açorda	Bread and garlic soup
Caldo verde	Portuguese kale soup
Sopa de legumes	Vegetable soup
Sopa de peixe	Fish soup
Sopa alentejana	Garlic soup with egg
Amêijoas	Cockles
Azeitonas	Olives
Caracóis	Snails
Espargos frios	Cold asparagus
Melão com presunto	Melon with ham
Pão com manteiga	Bread and butter
Salada de atum	Tuna salad
Salada à portuguesa	Mixed salad
Sardinhas em azeite	Sardines in olive oil

Peixe e mariscos/Fish and seafood

Amêijoas ao natural	Cockles
Atum	Tuna
Bacalhau com todos	Codfish with garnish
Bacalhau à bráz	Codfish, fried potato, scrambled egg
Caldeirada	Fish stew
Camarão grelhado	Grilled shrimps
Cataplana	Mussels, fish or meat, paprika, onion, potato
Dourada	Sea bream
Ensopado de enguias	Eel stew
Espadarte	Swordfish
Filetes de cherne	Fillet of grouper
Gambas na grelha	Grilled prawns
Lagosta cozida	Boiled lobster
Linguado	Sole
Lulas à sevilhana	Baked squid
Mêilhões de cebolada	Mussels with onions
Pargo	Snapper
Peixe espada	Scabbard fish
Perca	Perch
Pescada à portuguesa	Hake, Portuguese style

Salmão	Salmon
Sardinhas assadas	Grilled sardines

Carne e aves/Meat and poultry

Bife à portuguesa	Portuguese beefsteak
Bife de cebolada	Steak with onion
Bife de peru	Turkey steak
Cabrito	Kid
Carne de porco à Alentejana	Pork with cockles
Carne na grelha/Churrasco	Charcoal-grilled meat
Coelho	Rabbit
Costeleta de cordeiro	Lamb chop
Costeleta de porco	Pork chop
Escalope de vitela	Veal cutlet
Espetadas de carne	Meat skewer
Fígado de vitela	Calf's liver
Frango assado	Roast chicken
Frango na púcara	Chicken casserole
Iscas	Braised liver
Lebre	Hare
Leitão assado	Roast suckling pig
Lombo de carneiro	Mutton back
Pato	Duck
Perdiz	Partridge
Pimentões recheados	Stuffed peppers
Porco assado	Roast pork
Rins	Kidneys
Tripas	Tripe

Legumes/Vegetables

Batatas	Potatoes
Beringelas fritas	Fried aubergine
Bróculos	Broccoli
Cogumelos	Mushrooms
Espargos	Asparagus
Espinafres	Spinach
Feijão verde	Green beans
Pepinos	Gherkins

Sobremesa/Dessert

Arroz doce	Rice pudding
Gelado misto	Ice cream
Leite creme	Crème caramel

Pêra Helena	Pear belle Hélène
Pudim flan	Pudding with caramel sauce
Sorvete	Sorbet
Tarte de amêndoa	Almond cake

Lista de bebidas/List of beverages

Aguardente de figos/velho	Fig/old brandy
Bagaço	Bagasse brandy
Ginjinha	Cherry liqueur
Madeira	Madeira wine
Medronho	Strawberry tree brandy
Porto	Port wine
Cerveja/Imperial	Beer/draught beer
Caneca	large draught beer
Vinho branco/Vinho tinto	White wine/red wine
Vinho verde	Light wine with natural acidity
Água mineral	Mineral water
Bica	Espresso
Café (com leite)	Coffee (with milk)
Chá com leite/limão	Tea with milk/lemon
Galão	Milky coffee in a glass
Meia de leite	Coffee with lots of milk
Garoto	Espresso with milk
Laranjada/Sumo de laranja	Orangeade/Orange juice

Accommodation

Could you please recommend?	Se faz favor, pode recomendarme
...a good hotel/a guesthouse	um bom hotel?/uma pensão?
Do you still have a room free?	Ainda tem quartos livres?
a single room	um quarto individual
a double room	um quarto de casal
a twin bed room	um quarto con duas camas
with bathroom	com casa de banho
for one night/week.	para uma noite/semana.

Doctor/Bank/Post office

Can you recommend a good doctor?	Pode indicar-me um bom médico?
It hurts here.	Dói-me aqui.
Is there a bank here?	Onde há aqui um banco?
Postage stamps	selo

| How much does a letter/a postcard cost to England? | Quanto custa um postal/uma carta para a Inglaterra? |

Numbers

0	zero
1	um, uma
2	dois, duas
3	três
4	quatro
5	cinco
6	seis
7	sete
8	oito
9	nove
10	dez
11	onze
12	doze
13	treze
14	catorze
15	quinze
16	dezasseis
17	dezassete
18	dezoito
19	dezanove
20	vinte
30	trinta
40	quarenta
50	cinquenta
60	sessenta
70	setenta
80	oitenta
90	noventa
100	cem
101	cento e um
200	duzentos
1000/2000	mil/dois mil
1/2	um meio
1/3	um terço
1/4	um quarto

Days of the week

Segunda-feira	Monday
Terça-feira	Tuesday

Quarta-feira	Wednesday
Quinta-feira	Thursday
Sexta-feira	Friday
Sábado	Saturday
Domingo	Sunday
Feriado	Holiday

Literature

Christopher Columbus: *Logbook*. Penguin Classics, 1992 For anyone wishing to delve deeper into the voyages of discovery of Christopher Columbus.

Background information **John and Pat Underwood**: *Madeira: Car Tours and Walks*, Sunflower Books 2010. 10th edition of a classic guide to walking on the island.

Gerald Luckhurst: *The Gardens of Madeira*, Frances Lincoln 2010 30 gardens on the island, described by an expert.

Tony Clarke: *Field Guide to the Birds of the Atlantic Islands*, A&C Black, 2006. Up-to-date work describing all species found on the Macaronesian islands, i.e. the Canaries, Madeira, Azores and Cape Verde.

Marcus Binney: *The Blandys of Madeira: 1811-2011*, Frances Lincoln 2011. 200 years of a company and family that has shaped the history of the island and its famous wine.

Fiction **Jim Williams:** *Tango in Madeira*, Marble City 2014. After WWI the fates of several famous people become entwined in a mystery cum historical novel.

Media

Radio and television Most hotels and apartments receive **foreign-language channels**. **Portuguese television** comprises two state channels, RTP 1 and 2 (culture), as well as various private stations such as SIC and TVI. Foreign films are usually broadcast in their original language with subtitles.

Newspapers and magazines English daily newspapers and weekly magazines can be purchased at virtually every newsstand or kiosk in Funchal, as well as in many hotels. Daily papers tend to arrive on the island a day after publication, however.

Visitors to Madeira will find **Soft Madeira News Magazine and Madeira Life**, published in English, of interest. The latter incorporates listings for forthcoming events over the next couple of months, a basic bus timetable and useful telephone numbers (taxi, hospital, police station). Madeira's daily newspapers are the *Jornal da Madeira* and *Diário de Notícias* with a weather chart, cruise ship timetables and useful telephone numbers.

Money

Since 2002, the euro has been legal tender. Coins show the royal seal of 1134 (1/2/5 cent), of 1142 (10/20/50 cent) and of 1144 (€1/2).

Euro

Banks are open Mon – Fri 8.30am – 5pm, although many close for lunch between 12.30pm and 2pm.

Banks

The easiest way to pick up cash is from a cash machine (ATM) (»Multibanco«, maximum €200), with instructions in several languages. ATMs are widely distributed, also in smaller villages; they can now be used for electronic transfers as well. EC cards (standard charge approx. €4), bank cards and credit cards (using the latter can be very expensive!) are all accepted in conjunction with a PIN number. Banks, the larger hotels, high-class restaurants, car rental companies and some of the bigger specialist stores accept most internationally recognized credit cards. Visa and Eurocard are widespread, American Express and Diners Club less so.

Cash machines, credit cards

Post and Communications

Post offices can be identified by the sign »correio« (Portuguese for post office). Opening hours are usually Mon – Fri 9am – 12.30pm and 2.30pm – 6pm. The post office in the Avenida Zarco in the centre of Funchal is open all day Mon – Fri 9am – 8pm and 9am – 6pm on Saturdays and Sundays.

Post offices

For letters (*cartas*) and postcards (*postais*) within Europe, postage costs 70 cents. (*selos*) can be purchased in post offices or in shops bearing the sign »CTT Selos«. Allow around a week for letters and postcards to reach their destination. The more expensive »correio azul« is somewhat faster.

Postage

Public telephones | Almost all public telephones on Madeira have been converted from coin-operated models to telephone cards (»Telecom Card« or »cartão para telefonar«), which can be purchased in post offices or kiosks.

Mobile phones | Mobile telephones (*telemóvel*) will automatically access the local roaming partner. Locally bought prepaid cards or chips can be less expensive. Network coverage is good in urban areas, but less reliable in the more remote regions. No international dialling code is required, just add 291 before the number you wish to call. To call a mobile phone, just dial the nine-digit number.

FROM MADEIRA/ PORTO SANTO
to Canada/USA
tel. 001

to United Kingdom
tel. 0044

to Ireland
tel. 00353

The zero of the local code should be omitted.

TO MADEIRA/ PORTO SANTO
From outside Portuguese territory
tel. 00351 followed by the nine digit number, which begins with 291 on Madeira and Porto Santo.

Prices and Discounts

Tipping | In cafés and bars it is customary to leave a few coins on the table or on the counter, whilst in restaurants a tip of between 5% and 10% is appropriate. At the end of a taxi ride, round up the amount accordingly. Chambermaids, porters or tourist guides on sightseeing trips will appreciate a tip of two or three euros.

As part of a project subsidized by the EU »Um computador para todos« (A Computer for Everyone) free **public WLAN** zones were set up in all of the administrative districts of Madeira (Infos at www.wifi-madeira.com and http://espaconet.madeiratecnopolo.pt).

? MARCO ⊕ POLO INSIGHT

What does it cost?

Simple double room: from €30
Three-course meal: from €18
Simple meal: €8
Glass of beer: from €1
Espresso: from €0.70
Bus ride: from €1.25

▶ Prices for restaurants: p. 6
▶ Prices for hotel rooms: p. 6

Eco-Bus | The Eco-Bus runs free in the city of Funchal. The line runs in two loops between the two outer riverbeds, through streets including Rua da Carreira, Rua Aljube (north of the cathedral) and Rua Ornelas (to the market hall). Operating times: Mon to Fri 7.30am – 8pm, Sat

7.30am – 2pm, every 30 minutes except during midday (info at www.horariosdofunchal.pt).

A multi-day pass for the yellow city buses in Funchal mit be worthwhile (in case the Eco-Bus isn't running at the desired times); a three-day-ticket costs €11.30, for 5 days €15.50. They can be bought at reduced prices at the street kiosks (be persistent when asking for them!).
Individual bus tickets can also be bought at the kiosks for less than when buying them directly from the bus driver: €1.25 instead of €1.95

Multi-day pass

Parking in **parking zones 5 and 6** (farther from the terminal) at the airport is free for the first 45 minutes; afterwards it costs €0.25 per quarter hour; right in front of the terminal parking for a quarter hour costs €0.50 (Infos auf www.anam.pt).

Cheap parking

The MadeiraCard, which costs €12.50 and which is valid for a calendar year, entitles the owner to discounts of 5 to 25 % or little »extras« in restaurants, cafés, bars, museums, guided tours etc. The card can be purchased in Funchal in the Madeira Story Centre, at Madeira Wine, in the larger hotels or by telephone under tel. 2 91 10 58 44 (Info at www.madeiracard.com).

MadeiraCard

Some restaurants around Funchal offer free dinner transfers on a (mini-) bus – e. g. the »Vila do Peixe« in ▶ Câmara de Lobos (tel. 2 91 09 99 09, www.viladopeixe.com).

Free dinner transfer

Time

Madeira, like the Portuguese mainland, observes Western European Time (WET = Greenwich Mean Time). Summer time also applies from the end of March until the end of October, so visitors from Britain need not reset their watches.

Madeira and the Portuguese mainland

Toilets

At the beaches on Madeira (e.g. in Ponta do Sol, Madalena do Mar, Riberia Brava), but also at Prainha Beach and in Machico there are public toilets at an international standard and usually in good condition. The same applies for the WCs in large shopping centres. Generally even non-customers are allowed to use the »banheiro« or (»casa de«) »banho« in any bar when they ask politely. In smaller cafés or restaurants there is often only one unisex toilet.

Transport

DRIVING

Traffic regulations On Madeira – as in the rest of Portugal – vehicles drive on the right. Within urban areas, the speed limit is 50kmh/31mph; elsewhere on trunk roads the maximum is 90kmh/56 mph, rising to 100kmh/62mph on fast roads. The wearing of seat belts is compulsory. Children up to 12 years must sit in the back. Motorcyclists must wear a helmet. Telephoning is only permitted with a hands-free system. Driving with a blood alcohol level of 0.5 millilitres or more is an offence. A hi-visibility vest and warning triangle must be kept in the vehicle.

Road conditions Madeira meanwhile has a well-developed system of motorways with lots of tunnels and some bridges, which replace the previous curves and bottlenecks and make for relaxed driving. Some of the old roads are now only one way roads. But it is still better for drivers who do not know Madeira to **drive carefully**. Madeirans tends to drive fast on straight roads and to make risky passing manoeuvres. Moreover, away from the more populated areas there are still narrow village and mountain roads, which are often steep and have limited visibility. Care is of essence after village festivals. Mud slides after strong rains can also cause unexpected hindrances on side roads.

Petrol There are plenty of petrol stations in Funchal, but not so many further away. Most petrol stations are open until 10pm, some until midnight. Lead-free petrol is available as »gasolina sem chumbo 95« and »gasolina sem chumbo 98«.

> **? MARCO ⊕ POLO INSIGHT**
>
> *Reflective vest*
>
> A reflective warning vest must be worn on leaving a vehicle in the case of breakdown or an accident. Check if one is present in rental vehicles – otherwise, a €60 fine may be incurred!

The cost of **rental cars** varies with the season, car model and rental agency (local agencies are usually cheaper, as is reserving the car online in advance) between €27 and €95 per day. There is usually a surcharge for returning a rental car at a location other than the pick-up location.

A valid driving licence is required and the minimum age for drivers is 21. Rental companies often insist on 12 months driving experience. Third-party insurance is statutory, comprehensive cover is recommended. If any problems arise with the vehicle, check with the rental company. In the event of an accident, contact the police.

RENTAL CAR
LOCAL AGENTS
Rodavante
Aeroporto da Madeira
tel. 291 524 718, fax 291 524 762
Aeroporto do Porto Santo
tel. 291 982 925
Estr. Monumental
306 Hotel Florasol, Funchal
tel. 291 764 361, www.rodavante.com

Moinho
Hotel Vila Baleira Loja 1, Porto Santo
tel. 291 982 141 Fax 291 982 717
Aeroporto de Porto Santo
tel. 291 983 260
moinho@moinho-rentacar.com
www.moinhorentacar.com

Magoscar
Caniço: Apartado 46
tel. 291 934 818
www.magoscar.com

INTERNATIONAL
Avis
tel. (UK) 08700 100 287
www.avis.com
Funchal Airport
tel. 291 524 392

Europcar
tel. (UK) 08713 849 847
www.europcar.co.uk
Funchal Airport
tel. 2 91 52 46 33

Hertz
tel. (UK 24hrs) 0843 309 3009
www.hertz.co.uk
Funchal Airport
tel. 291 42 63 00

Sixt
tel. 2 91 52 33 55
(Funchal Airport)
www.sixt.co.uk

Madeiran taxis are yellow. Taxi rides are not too expensive, but be-   Taxi
ware of some rather imaginative prices, particularly in Funchal. A list
of set journey prices on the island is available, with taxi ranks located
on the square in front of the town hall, for example, and on the Avenida Arriaga by the Jardim Municipal.
Longer excursions with a taxi are also a possibility. Take a ride to the
beginning of a levada hike, for instance, and arrange a collection at
the destination.

PUBLIC TRANSPORT

Madeira's public transport network is relatively well developed, if   In Funchal
somewhat complex. Funchal's municipal bus service is generally ef-   and across
ficient. Buses (autocarros) go to all places on the island, sometimes   the country
admittedly at snail's pace. Careful planning is necessary, as in some
cases services to the more remote spots run only once per day. Six
private bus companies are based in Funchal. They have various different points of departure, although most start from the Avenida do

Mar. Funchal has **no central bus station**. Take care to note the destination as marked on the bus, as the municipal and cross-country services sometimes use the same numbers! Almost all bus routes are out of service on 25 December and, to a slightly lesser extent, on 31 December. Departure times, timetables and further details can be obtained from the tourist information offices. The plan for Funchal indicates routes to the most important tourist spots. For journeys within Funchal, a multi-day pass (▶p. 225) is worth considering for those not living immediately in the centre. On **Porto Santo**, four bus routes depart daily from Vila Baleira to various places on the island. **Bus stops** are usually, but not always, marked by a »paragem« sign – in isolated locations, some detective work may be required. Timetables and departure times are displayed at bus stops – depending on the bus company, departure times from the starting point of the route may also be listed. It is advisable to signal to the bus to stop, otherwise it may simply drive past.

Selected bus routes

HORÁRIOS DE FUNCHAL
www.horariosdofunchal.pt

Routes 1, 2 4 – Eco Line (linha verde)
Intra-urban routes to the hotel zone

Line 56
Funchal – Santana

Line 77
Funchal – Santo da Serra

Line 81
Funchal – Curral das Freiras

Line 103
Funchal – Arco S. Jorge

Line 113
Funchal – Camacha/Santa Cruz

Line 138
Funchal – São Jorge

RODOESTE
www.rodoeste.pt

Line 4
Funchal – Ponta do Sol

Line 6
Funchal – Arco de São Jorge

Line 7
Funchal – Ribeira Brava

Line 8
Funchal – Madalena do Mar

Line 80
Funchal – Porto Moniz via Calheta

Line 96
Funchal – Corrida, Jardim da Serra

Line 115
Funchal – Estreito da Calheta

Line 123
Funchal – Campanário

Travellers with Disabilities

On account of its topography, Madeira is rather **difficult terrain** for travellers with disabilities. The steep paths and roads and a proliferation of cobblestones make the going tough, not just for the wheelchair-bound. To date, few hotels have full accessibility facilities. The situation is improving, albeit relatively slowly. Levada hikes are nigh on impossible for those with limited mobility, as the trails are usually far too narrow. On the plus side, a **hiking trail through the laurisilva forest** from Pico das Pedras to Queimadas, almost 2 km/over a mile long, has been made suitable for wheelchairs.

When to Go

Thanks to its favourable climate and mild temperatures, the island is worth a visit at any time of year. Even in winter, temperatures only drop to European levels in the upper regions of the island, whilst in Funchal, for example, the thermometer rarely dips below 18°C/64°F (▶ p. 19).

An island for any time of year

With Madeira being such a popular **summer** destination not only for sunseeking Europeans, but also for the Portuguese themselves, the island is undeniably busy during the Portuguese summer holidays, but never overcrowded. Nevertheless, if at all possible avoid July and August, especially on the neighbouring island of Porto Santo with its long stretches of sandy beach. The peak season on Madeira also encompasses the week from **Christmas** to **New Year**. The island is busier in this period and prices somewhat higher.

High season

From April to June and again from September until the beginning of November, which are the low seasons, there are considerably fewer visitors. But in these times as well the island is in full bloom, while the sun is less intense.

Low season

Although Madeira is **in bloom all year round**, it is good to know what is blossoming on the island at any given time (▶ MARCO POLO Insight p.22/23). When the jacaranda trees reveal their violet blossoms in April / May, for example, Funchal looks particularly attractive. Roadsides and some of the levadas are adorned with blossoming hydrangeas and agapanthus in August / September. Camellia enthusiasts should come in winter.

Flowering island

Index

List of Maps and Illustrations

Photo Credits

Publisher's Information

1st Edition 2015
Worldwide Distribution: Marco Polo
Travel Publishing Ltd
Pinewood, Chineham Business Park
Crockford Lane, Chineham
Basingstoke, Hampshire RG24 8AL,
United Kingdom.

Photos, illlustrations, maps:
126 photos, 13 maps and illustrations,
one large map
Text: Rita Henss, Achim Bourmer, Heiner
F. Gstaltmayr, Dr. Eva Missler
Editing:
John Sykes, Rainer Eisenschmid
Translation: Patricia Aiken, Gareth
Davies, Barbara Schmidt-Runkel
Cartography:
Klaus-Peter Lawall, Unterensingen;
MAIRDUMONT Ostfildern (travel map)
3D illustrations:
jangled nerves, Stuttgart
Infographics:
Golden Section Graphics GmbH, Berlin
Design:
independent Medien-Design, Munich

Editor-in-chief:
Rainer Eisenschmid,
Mairdumont Ostfildern

Printed in China

Despite all of our authors' thorough
research, errors can creep in. The pub-
lishers do not accept any liability for thi
Whether you want to praise, alert us to
errors or give us a personal tip Please
contact us by email or post:

MARCO POLO Travel Publishing Ltd
Pinewood, Chineham Business Park
Crockford Lane, Chineham
Basingstoke, Hampshire RG24 8AL
United Kingdom
Email: sales@marcopolouk.com

FSC
www.fsc.org
MIX
Paper from
responsible sources
FSC® C011918

MARCO ⊕ POLO

HANDBOOKS

www.marco-polo.com

Madeira Curiosities

What to do in a storm, where the ukulele probably comes from, how the laurisilva forests grew – Madeira has some strange facts to offer.

►Liquid Antiques

The phylloxera aphids apparently thought that the white grape variety terrantez tastes especially delicious. In the 19th century they managed to decimate them almost completely. Currently there are terrantez wines from at least six producers available from the year 1795.

►Extensive Episcopal Powers

For almost forty years all of Brazil belonged to the bishopric of Funchal – the first Brazilian bishopric was only established in 1551 in Salvador de Bahia. For almost twenty years the powers of the chief shepherd of Madeira extended to the Cape Verde Islands and as far as Goa.

►Lordly Instrument

During her first stay on Madeira Austria's Empress Sisi posed for a photograph holding a braguinha. It is said that this small guitar-like instrument was the forerunner to the Hawaiian ukulele. An immigrant named João Fernandez is supposed to have brought a braguinha from Madeira to the Hawaiian Islands in the Pacific Ocean.

►Winged Seeds

Wild doves, say the experts, are responsible for the laurasilva woods on Madeira; they are supposed to have brought the seeds across the Atlantic Ocean. It is a fact that the endemic silver-necked dove looks like the two varieties of laurel pigeon on the Canary Islands. All of them commonly only digest the flesh of the laurasilva berries and not the seeds. These are then excreted – and become more or less the seed for a new laurasilva tree.

►Biscuit for Ships to Africa

The biscuits produced by the Fábrica de Santo Antonio in Funchal went down in nautical history. One variety – the Marias – were served with tea in the 1950s on the Africa route of the National Navigation Company. The »holy« Madeira baked goods were taken on board when the ocean-going giants stopped at Funchal.

►Mighty Lady in Heaven

Severe storms are not new to Madeira. In 1803 already after days of rain the rivers and streams in Funchal swelled, destroyed houses and carried people to their death. The islanders pleaded desperately with the Mother of God of Monte for help. A few hours later the heavens closed up – and Nossa Senhora do Monte became the patron saint of the whole island.